Pet Owner's Guide to
THE
YORKSHIRE TERRIER

Douglas McKay

NEW YORK

HOWELL BOOK HOUSE
A Prentice Macmillan Company
15 Columbus Circle
New York, NY 10023

MACMILLAN is a registered trademark of Macmillan, Inc.

Library of Congress Cataloging-in-Publication data

McKay, Douglas.
  Pet owner's guide to the Yorkshire terrier / by Douglas McKay.
1st American ed.
     p.   cm.
  ISBN 0-87605-993-0
  1. Yorkshire terriers.   I. Title
SF429.Y6M25   1994   94-9535   CIP
636.7'6 – dc20

Manufactured in Hong Kong
10 9 8 7 6 5 4 3 2 1

Contents

The Yorkshire Terrier is acknowledged worldwide as the most glamorous of all Toy dogs.

Dedication

This book is dedicated to the memory of two devoted companions, our Milly (Nelmila Berryfield Opal) and the most beautiful Nicky Girl, whose love and loyalty were the inspiration and reward for our efforts

About the author

Douglas McKay has been involved with dogs all his life, and for the last twenty years he has specialised in Yorkshire Terriers, breeding, exhibiting and judging this enchanting toy breed. In partnership with his wife Hannah, he has made up a number of Champions under his Clantalon prefix, including a Crufts CC winner, who went on to become the breed CC recordholder for Scotland. When this male was used for breeding his offspring included a Champion daughter, the top UK puppy in the breed for 1988, and another Champion son, who was a Crufts CC winner in 1991, top male in the breed 1991-1992, Crufts Reserve CC winner in 1992, Scottish Show Dog of the Year finalist in 1991, and Reserve Show Dog of the Year All Breeds in Scotland, 1992. Douglas is a Championship show judge, he is involved in show administration, and is President and Chairman of the Yorkshire Terrier Club of Scotland.

Acknowledgements

I acknowledge the help and forebearance of my wife Hannah and my daughter Karen. My thanks for the invaluable photographic and artistic contribution of Jean Halliday, Sandra Arroya, Brian Downey, and Sandra Russell of Russell Fine Arts.

Cover picture: Courtesy of Joan Gordon.

Photography: Carol Ann Johnson

Chapter One

EARLY HISTORY

ORIGINS

Britain is the home of the Yorkshire Terrier, and while much has been written regarding the origins of this delightful and glamorous little Toy dog, opinions vary as to the development of the breed prior to the first recognised show classes held at Birmingham in 1862. The 'new' breed was scheduled under the heading 'Broken Haired Terriers', and included dogs subsequently identified in the Kennel Club Stud Book as Yorkshire Terriers.

Prior to this time there existed a profusion of terrier types exhibited under the various headings of 'Scotch' and 'Broken Haired Terriers' in classes frequently defined by weight. These were predominantly the Clydesdale Terrier, the Paisley Terrier and the Skye Terrier, all originating, as their names imply, in these areas of Scotland. Many of these terriers found their way south to England at the time of the Industrial Revolution. This was because the Scottish mining and textile workers from the Clyde Valley migrated, in search of work, to the mills and mines of Lancashire and Yorkshire.

The Skye Terrier came originally from the Isle of Skye, off the west coast of Scotland, and weighed between 16-20lbs (7.3-9k). The breed was noted for a long back, a flat, harsh topcoat with an undercoat, and was used for badger baiting. The urban Clydesdale Terrier and Paisley Terriers were kept as pets and used for rat catching by the miners and mill workers of these areas. Both resembled a smaller type Skye Terrier with erect ears, shorter back, and a much longer, silky coat. The Clydesdale was a dark steel-blue and tan, while the Paisley was a lighter blue. Both weighed between 12 and 15lbs (5.4-6.8k). It was, therefore, essentially a transition from these Scottish Terriers to the Yorkshire Terrier, as they were all similar in most respects to the Yorkie we know today.

It was inevitable that these dogs would be interbred in Lancashire and Yorkshire with the indigenous population of animals, which were the Manchester Terrier, the Black and Tan Terrier, the Halifax Fawn and the Silky Terrier, all of which have been credited with playing a significant part in the foundation of the Yorkshire Terrier. It has even been suggested that the Maltese, that most exotic little creature with a pure white coat and a pedigree of antiquity, has at various times been interbred with the Yorkie to improve the quality and texture of the Yorkie coat.

THE FIRST DESIGNER DOG

The Yorkshire Terrier did not simply evolve as some happy accident of fate; it was probably the first 'designer dog' to be deliberately produced. The breed evolved over a relatively short time, with the specific aim of creating a small, fearless but glamorous Toy dog, with a long silky coat of contrasting colours.

It certainly suited the miners and mill workers to have a very small, yet courageous dog, as both dog and master were forced to live and work in rat-infested conditions of extreme deprivation. The working man not only required a dog for companionship, he also needed a good ratter capable of killing the rats which plagued his working environment. There was also the chance of the dog making a modest financial contribution by competing in the public house rat-pit, where the dogs would kill rats and their owners would gamble on the outcome. Therefore, a good dog of this type was a valuable and much sought-after commodity, and could change hands for a substantial amount.

MINIATURE DOGS

The first formally organised dog shows, which began in England in 1859, were to coincide with the fashionable Victorian demand for miniature dogs. The Yorkshireman, shrewd and quick to seize the opportunity to supplement his meagre income, very quickly recognised the potential of this new fad, and quickly bred his terrier down in size to accommodate the demand. Before long, a dog which had been a ratter weighing about 12-15lbs (5.4-6.8k) was reduced to 8-10lbs (3.6-4.5k). Soon specimens of between 3-5lbs (1.4-2.3k) were not only showing and winning, but also becoming increasingly popular as pets, selling for considerable sums of money to the more affluent Victorians in London and the South.

THE FATHER OF THE BREED

Credit for inventing the Yorkshire Terrier breed goes to a gentleman called Peter Eden, of Manchester. He was a notable dog and terrier man of his day, greatly respected as a judge, officiating at many of the prestigious official shows formally recognised by the newly-formed Kennel Club. Mr Eden had a number of excellent specimens, with long, silky coats of blue and tan, which he regularly and successfully exhibited. He is credited with the first entry of a Yorkshire Terrier in the Kennel Club Stud Book. First published in 1874, this included all dogs registered prior to that date, and it is here under the heading of 'Broken Haired Scotch and Yorkshire Terriers' that we find the entry for Mr Eden's 'Albert', who was to feature so prominently on both sides of the pedigree of Mr and Mrs Jonas Foster's famous 'Huddersfield Ben'.

HUDDERSFIELD BEN

Huddersfield Ben was famous for his show ring wins, and was therefore in great demand as a stud dog. History shows that he was certainly prolific in passing on his qualities to many of his offspring – there can be no question that nearly every Yorkie can trace its origins to this particular dog.

Huddersfield Ben was born in 1865, bred and owned by a Mr Eastwood of Huddersfield, a publican, who specifically bred the dog to compete in the rat-pits in his public house. Ben did this successfully for the first three years of his life until his rescue, when he was found and purchased by Mr and Mrs Jonas Foster. His show career was short but distinguished, ended by his untimely death in a road accident when he was only six and a half years old.

In this very short span of time, he was able to leave an indelible mark on the

The Skye Terrier was one of the small terrier breeds to play a significant part in the development of the Yorkshire Terrier.

The Yorkie was bred to be a top-class ratter, with the skill and courage to kill the rats which plagued his owner's working environment.

Today the Yorkie is the show dog par excellence, with his stunning full coat. But this extrovert little dog also makes a superb pet.

history of the breed by the amazing feat of having thirty of his offspring registered in the Kennel Club Stud Book. Huddersfield Ben was undoubtedly the Yorkshire Terrier who most closely resembled the breed as we see it today, and whilst he was a larger dog at 12lbs (5.5k), his offspring were principally of a smaller size.

BRADFORD HARRY

The second half of the 19th century saw the birth of the breed as we know it today. Huddersfield Ben's tremendous influence resulted in a new and rapidly expanding family of Yorkshire Terrier enthusiasts extending the length and breadth of Britain – all in the span of thirty years from 1860 to 1890. In 1880 the first export of the breed arrived in the United States, and the first Champion to gain his title in America was an English export, Bradford Harry, a grandson of the legendary Huddersfield Ben.

The early 1900s saw increasing popularity of the breed, both in Britain and the USA. Many quality dogs were exported from the top breeders in Britain in the immediate pre- and post-war years, forming the foundation of many of the American and Canadian bloodlines that we recognise today. The Second World War brought breeding to a virtual standstill in Britain, but the important kennels that managed to keep going found a ready market for their puppies in America.

THE BREED SPREADS

Following the Second World War, Yorkshire Terrier enthusiasts took little time in making up lost ground, and by 1945 the breed was once again on its feet. The number of registrations rocketed, fuelled by a seemingly insatiable demand from Europe and the Far East, where the dog world had discovered the attractions and the qualities of the glamorous Yorkie, plus a continuing demand for quality stock from North America. There can be little doubt that today, there is a nucleus of both pet and show quality Yorkies in almost every civilised country in the world.

Chapter Two

CHOOSING A PUPPY

WHY A YORKIE?

There are many excellent benefits to sharing your life with a Yorkshire Terrier. In addition to the rewards of pleasure and companionship, young children have the opportunity to learn that love and affection go with tolerance and understanding of their fellow creatures. The companionship of a small dog can also have a regenerative and therapeutic effect on the lives of the elderly, the lonely or the sick, by giving a sense of purpose, while the Yorkie's bark can be a significant deterrent to potential intruders.

The Yorkshire Terrier is a fearless Toy Terrier, with an adaptable temperament that is compatible with an urban environment or equal to a rural existence. Being small of stature, the Yorkie does not require a great deal of space or exercise, and is therefore well suited to the circumstances of town life. He will happily adjust to his owner's lifestyle, and while comfortable in the larger family with children, he is also perfectly content with the elderly and those living alone.

The Yorkie can best be described as a 'character'; not always modest, he imagines himself to be of greater stature than his appearance portrays. He has an engaging personality, with a sound, friendly temperament and a cheerful disposition. He is, as a rule, easy to train, well-mannered and generally amenable to children and adults alike.

Being a small dog, upkeep is not expensive, although a Yorkie will require a booster injection once a year to protect him against the major infectious diseases. Feeding is not expensive, as a Yorkie will happily consume the same food as the rest of the family, if required. The other bonus is that the Yorkie does not cast his coat as do most breeds. While this might be an important factor for the house-proud, it can also be an advantage for those unable to keep a dog because of an allergic reaction to the dog hair.

BUYING A PUPPY

It is sensible to consider your present circumstances and future plans so as to be confident that these are compatible with ownership of, and responsibility for, a dog. For example, if you are thinking of moving house, travelling, starting a family, or if you need to go into hospital in the near future, it might be sensible to wait until things are more settled before taking on the extra commitment of a puppy.

The most common mistake people make when buying a puppy is failing to consider the implications of taking on such a major long-term commitment, not only for themselves but for the other members of the household. It is therefore important

Many people fall in love with the idea of owning a beautiful long-coated Yorkie, but the coat takes time to grow, and a lot of hard work goes into maintaining a dog in full coat. The puppy on the left is eight months old, and his coat is just beginning to grow in length.

At eight weeks of age the puppies should have a short, glossy black body-coat with tan points clearly visible on the face, chest and legs. The eyes should be dark and sparkling.

Yorkies do vary in size, and if you have young children in your family, it may be advisable to choose a dog from a line which produces slightly bigger, more robust puppies.

to consult with those who will be affected by this proposed addition to the family, before bringing a puppy into your home and heart.

Make your plans, taking advantage of the available expertise relevant to this important event. In this way you will derive the maximum benefit from your puppy and will be well rewarded for your effort with love and loyalty which, hopefully, will endure for some fifteen years – the reasonable life expectancy of a Yorkshire Terrier.

The best way of locating a suitable puppy will depend on your particular requirements. For example, you may simply want a dog as companion, and while that is an important reason to be careful and patient about your purchase, you may require a different strategy if you are going to start breeding Yorkshire Terriers, or if you want to buy a puppy in order to compete in the show ring. Do not be in a hurry to buy the first puppy you encounter, as there is much to consider before producing your cheque book.

SIZE

In spite of being a Toy breed the Yorkie is still a terrier, and so size is an important consideration, as there can be a significant variation in size and weight. Yorkies can be as small as 2-3lbs (0.9-1.4k) in weight, ranging up to as much as 10-12lbs (4.5-5.4k). Therefore, it is important to ascertain the potential size of your prospective puppy. As a rule, the smaller in size are better suited to the mature owner, or those living alone. It is not always a good idea to consider a 'tiny' if there are very young children in the family. Accidents are best avoided, and small dogs and small children are not always compatible when there is the ever-present danger of a small dog being trodden on, tripped over, or shut in a door.

COAT

While it is an excellent idea to visit a show before you buy your puppy, many people become over-enthusiastic or unrealistic about their own aspirations when they first encounter the captivating appearance of a show Yorkie in full coat. You cannot instantly buy a puppy that looks like this, and it is not just a matter of waiting until the coat grows. It takes a great deal of experience, and several years of selfless dedicated work, on a daily basis, to lovingly tend, nurture and look after the coat of the show Yorkie.

It is a labour of love to achieve this appearance, and not something to which everyone is best-suited. In any event, it is not to be undertaken lightly by the uninitiated. Neither should you be deterred by this glamorous appearance, as it is quite appropriate for the pet Yorkie to be kept trimmed in a suitably smart, but more manageable short style.

MALE OR FEMALE

There is not really much difference in temperament between the sexes in this breed. It is interesting to note that for a male to be smaller than a bitch is not only acceptable, but desirable. However, there is little point in buying a male puppy, if your aim is to breed Yorkshire Terriers. If this is your plan, you should be looking for a well-bred bitch puppy who is a typical specimen of the breed.

If you do buy a bitch, and you do not plan to breed a litter, you must be prepared to cope with the amorous attentions of male dogs in the neighbourhood when your bitch is in season, which usually happens twice a year. The option is to have your bitch spayed, which puts an end to this type of problem.

FINDING A BREEDER
Obviously, you want to purchase a healthy puppy who has been carefully reared in the first weeks of life by a caring and responsible breeder. The first step is to write to your national Kennel Club, and they will provide you with the name and address of the secretary of your local Yorkshire Terrier Club. The secretary will give you advice regarding suitable stock, and will put you in touch with breeders in your area.

One of the advantages of buying from a show exhibitor is that it is in the best interests of the exhibitor to breed from not only the best, but the soundest stock available. Breeder-exhibitors will have knowledge of their own stock, and will have a fair idea whether they are likely to be able to provide something suitable to your requirements. Do not be in the least surprised or offended if you are, at some point, interrogated in some detail by the breeder regarding your suitability as a dog owner and your circumstances. A conscientious breeder will want to be satisfied about the kind of home a precious puppy is going into, before entrusting it to your care.

ASSESSING THE PUPPIES
Now the big moment has arrived: you have located a breeder with a litter of puppies available. You have examined Yorkies in general and know what you like, but how do you go about choosing a puppy? The best plan is to put yourself in the breeder's hands and trust their experience, as the Yorkie pup at this age bears very little resemblance to the mature adult.

A responsible breeder will not want to bring a stranger in to view or handle the puppies before their eyes are open, and when they are still entirely dependant on their mother. This is because it could upset the mother, and there is a risk of introducing infection. The breeder will not want to part with puppies until they are fully weaned; most will be happy to sell pups from eight to twelve weeks of age.

It is always good manners to make an appointment in advance to see a litter of puppies. When you arrive, the unspoken rule is to look, but do not touch the puppies without first asking or being invited. The general environment should be clean and tidy, and sweet-smelling – cleanliness is indeed next to godliness as far as looking after livestock is concerned.

It is always a good idea to see puppies at feeding time when they are likely to be at their most active. This is the best time to identify the puppy with a healthy appetite and good temperament, for a good eater is likely to thrive and be more resistant to illness and infection than the one with a poor appetite. It is quite natural for a puppy to be boisterous and assertive and it is an acceptable part of normal development that they should exercise by pulling one another about. Nevertheless, it is inadvisable to choose a puppy who appears hyper-active, or over-aggressive, in comparison with the rest of the litter. Equally, it is a mistake to pick the puppy who sits alone and forlorn in the corner, just because he has an appealing look and you feel sorry for him.

At this age, the Yorkie puppy should have a short, glossy, black body-coat with tan points clearly defined above the eyes, on the chest and on the legs, around the breech and on the underside of the tail. The eyes should be dark and sparkling, and clean, white teeth are indicative of good health. The nose should be cool, moist and free of discharge, but remember there are times when a puppy's nose can be dry and warm, and the pup is in good health. The ears should be small and preferably erect, or small enough to look as though they will eventually stand up, and they should be clean and dry, both inside and out.

You will want to see the puppies' mother, but do not be too critical if she appears out of condition. This is only to be expected after giving birth and looking after her puppies, but you should still be able to get a good idea of her type and temperament. It is also important to establish whether the breeder has knowledge of any hereditary defects inherent in this particular breeding line, particularly with regard to slipping patella and hip dysplasia (See Chapter 9: Health Care), which is not uncommon in this breed.

PAPERWORK

Before you complete the transaction, it is important to come to some arrangement with the breeder about having a veterinary examination carried out, either immediately before the purchase is completed, or when you take the puppy for his first inoculations. If this reveals a previously undetected problem, it is important for everyone, not least the puppy, that this contingency forms part of the purchase contract.

When you take your puppy home, you should receive a copy of the pedigree, a diet sheet and possibly a sample of the recommended food, a record of worming carried out and the product used, and, finally, the Kennel Club registration papers.

Chapter Three

PUPPY CARE

PREPARATIONS
Planning and preparation are essential in order to integrate your puppy into his new home. If there are several people in the household, it is a good idea to let one person take overall responsibility for the new arrival. In the first few weeks this is especially important until a routine has been established, particularly with regard to feeding and house-training. The Yorkie is, generally, easy to train, but it is infinitely easier if the task is undertaken by the person most frequently in contact with the puppy at this critical time. It is also sensible to make a list of everything you might need for the arrival of the puppy.

SLEEPING QUARTERS
A bed of some kind is an essential requirement. A cardboard box – with a piece cut out to allow the puppy ease of access – is perfectly acceptable, although a small

Your puppy has a lot to get used to when he first arrives home.

nest-type bed is perhaps a more desirable acquisition. Most pet shops have a great variety of inexpensive beds, as well as small wicker ones which are slightly more expensive. There are more expensive multi-purpose travel boxes, which are highly recommended. These come in wood, wicker, plastic-wire, and they are rigid or collapsible in construction.

The base of the bed or box should be lined with newspaper, which insulates against the cold, and is disposable in the event of being accidentally soiled. Place something comfortable on top for the puppy to lie on. This can be a small blanket, or the fleecy type of dog bedding, which is machine washable.

You will also have to decide where the puppy is going to live and sleep when he does arrive. I recommend that the best place is in a quiet, warm, draught-free corner of the most used room in the house. This invariably turns out to be the kitchen/living room, which hopefully will have easy access to a garden area. Make sure that there is nothing within reach which your puppy can damage with his small but exceedingly sharp teeth. Likely attractions are stray wires and plugs, and other items of electrical equipment.

PLAY-PEN

It is wise to consider some kind of play-pen for your puppy, and, again, these are obtainable from a variety of sources: pet shops and accessory stalls at dog shows and even from garden centres. A pen is very useful, particularly if you have young children, as the puppy has a safe haven where he can sleep undisturbed. It also provides a place where your puppy can play with his toys etc, without being underfoot or getting up to mischief. The pen can be moved around the house, and into the garden when the weather allows. It is best to purchase a lightweight collapsible, portable mesh pen, with a non-toxic impervious coating.

COLLAR AND LEAD

You will also need a suitable collar and lead. To start with, you will need a soft 'cat' collar. The puppy will quickly grow out of this, and then you can choose from one of the range available in all pet shops. The lead should be leather, with a reasonably strong trigger hook for attaching it to the collar. Avoid harnesses altogether.

BRUSH AND COMB

You will need a baby brush, preferably bristle, and a fairly wide-toothed comb for regular grooming.

FEEDING BOWLS

Your puppy will require feeding bowls and a water dish. I recommend the stainless steel type, which are easy to keep clean, and which last for years.

TOYS

It is a good idea to buy a few indestructible toys and some puppy chews. Make sure they are completely safe, and that the puppy cannot chew bits off, which could cause problems if they were swallowed.

FINDING A VET

It is possible that you have owned an animal previously, in which case you may already have access to a vet that you know and have confidence in. You may have a friend who is very happy with a particular vet, or you may already have introduced yourself to a vet while looking for your puppy. If you are buying your puppy locally, then perhaps the breeder can recommend you to a vet who is familiar with and has experience of this particular line or Toy breeds generally.

I stress the importance of locating a vet before you need one, for even if the puppy has already had his first vaccinations you will want a general health check at an early date. This is also an ideal way of introducing yourself and your small charge to your vet, instead of waiting until you need to impose on him in an emergency.

Most vets are usually good all-rounders, but like doctors, there are sometimes specialists in group practice, and it is therefore wise to acquaint yourself with the small animal vet in the practice.

VACCINATIONS
In most cases your puppy will not have completed all his vaccinations before you get him, and this means your puppy cannot mix with other dogs until he has received full protection. There are differing views about the age at which the injections should be given, and there are also different types of vaccine available. However, these usually take the form of two separate injections given at different times, and these provide protection against the major infectious diseases of parvovirus, leptospirosis, distemper and hepatitis.

COLLECTING YOUR PUPPY
Once you have made all the necessary preliminary arrangements at home for the new arrival, you will need to make arrangements to collect the puppy. Try not to arrive at the kennels immediately after the puppy has been fed, as this could increase the possibility of car sickness. It is advisable to ask someone to come with you on the trip, either to drive, or to look after the puppy on the return journey.

Take a travelling box or basket if you can, and also something cosy to wrap the puppy in, especially if you are going to carry it in your arms. You would also be wise to take some paper towelling with you, should the puppy be car sick or relieve himself on the journey home.

ARRIVING HOME
The best time to introduce a puppy to your home is fairly early in the day to give him a chance to get acclimatised, and you should ensure that there is going to be someone at home for the remainder of the day. Resist the temptation of inviting visitors to come and look at your new puppy. This could add to the considerable stress that your new puppy is experiencing as a result of being suddenly relocated. It is a traumatic and disorientating experience for a youngster to be suddenly uprooted and to find himself in a strange new environment, and therefore it is very important that you do your best to minimise the anxiety associated with moving into a new home.

As soon as you get home, put the puppy in his new pen, lined with newspaper, and tempt him with a drink (water or milk, as advised by the breeder). Then give the new arrival the opportunity to relieve himself in the area that you intend using for that purpose. If the puppy has been accustomed to using newspaper in the breeder's premises, you can bring some newspaper from there, which will have a familiar

It is a good idea to introduce your puppy to his sleeping quarters at an early stage, so that he has a place where he can feel safe and secure.

A Yorkie puppy needs four meals a day until he is six to eight months of age.

The puppy coat is easy to maintain, as long as grooming is carried out on a regular, daily basis.

scent on it, as this can encourage the new arrival to re-establish his toilet routine more quickly, thus making life easier for everyone.

FEEDING
Puppies are normally weaned by the age of six weeks, and by the time your puppy arrives home he should be settled into a feeding routine, eating from a dish, and completely independent from his mother. It is important to establish from the breeder that weaning is complete, and to have detailed information concerning your puppy's current diet. For the first couple of weeks you should follow the routine as closely as possible, thus avoiding the risk of upsetting the puppy's digestion. Should it be necessary for you to alter the existing routine to suit your own circumstances, it is advisable to introduce change gradually.

Your puppy should be provided with three or four meals a day up to six to eight months of age, after which two to three meals a day should suffice. When the dog is mature, one main meal a day should be adequate. A plentiful supply of clean, fresh water should be accessible at all times to both puppy and adult dog alike, regardless of the feeding regime adopted by breeder or owner.

Always present food well broken down, as a small, greedy dog can very easily and quickly choke on a relatively small lump of food. If this happens, instant action is required to dislodge the obstruction by hooking it out with a finger, while avoiding pushing the obstruction further down the airway. If you fail to succeed, then turn the dog upside down and slap him vigorously on the back, or on both sides of the ribcage, and this may produce the desired effect.

THE FIRST NIGHT
The first night is the hardest part of acquiring a puppy, and the golden rule is to start as you mean to go on. Remember, this can be a distressing time for your puppy, who has just been separated from his family, and it is understandable that he might fret. While it may be tempting to put your puppy in with the children, it is not really such a good idea as it is not conducive to the discipline of the dog or the children, and plays havoc with attempts at house-training.

Your puppy should learn right from the beginning that he goes to bed in the sleeping quarters you have allocated. Additionally, it is worth placing a warm water-bottle underneath the bedding of a very young puppy, who will miss the comfort of sleeping with his littermates. A ticking clock, wrapped in a woollen, can be placed in close proximity to the puppy's bed. The ticking sound simulates the mother's heartbeat, and this may help the puppy to settle. You can also try leaving the radio on at a low volume to provide background noise, and you can leave a dimmed light on for the first few nights. If you are very lucky, your puppy may settle down immediately, but if he starts barking and whining, you should be prepared to tolerate this for a time. If it continues for any length of time, simply stand outside the door of the room containing the puppy (avoid entering the room, except as a last resort) and make a short, sharp, assertive noise of disapproval, and then leave the immediate area. If the puppy is extremely persistent, you may have to to repeat this exercise several times on different occasions before it is effective.

If you feel forced to submit and take the pup into the bedroom, it is essential to move the puppy complete with box and pen, in order to be able to relocate the pup at a more suitable stage in its development.

HOUSE TRAINING

It is essential to dispose of any overnight soiling first thing in the morning, before you do anything else. Then feed your puppy, and immediately take him out to the place you have allocated for his toilet. Stay with your puppy until he has performed, and then give lots of praise. This procedure should be followed at all feeding times, as a puppy will relieve himself immediately after being fed. The other times to be on the alert are every time your puppy wakes up, and after he has had a play session.

TEETHING

It is important to remember that your pup will be teething in the first year of his life and he will, from time to time, suffer considerable discomfort. As a result, he will be inclined to chew anything convenient, with sometimes catastrophic consequences if your most precious possessions happen to be lying about, or if loose wires are to hand. It is therefore essential to provide something suitable and safe, such as a rawhide chewstick, for the puppy to chew on while he is cutting teeth – and to make sure that everything dangerous or valuable is put out of reach.

There are several signs, apart from chewing, that will indicate that your puppy is teething. The gums may be sore and swollen, and the puppy may try to scratch or rub his face with either front or rear paws, or even rub the side of his face along the carpet or floor. This action should not be confused with the acceptable, but peculiar, burying action most Yorkies will engage in when saving a morsel of food. In this instance, a Yorkie may attempt to bury his 'treat' under a heap of non-existent earth in the middle of the room. During teething, the Yorkie's ears may drop from their usual erect position, and sometimes the ears do not go into their correct position until the teething process is complete.

When your Yorkie is teething, it is best to treat him as you would treat a baby in similar circumstances, and liberal application of teething-gel accompanied by tender loving care will bring some relief. In the worst cases, your puppy may run a temperature or have a headache and be light-sensitive. In this case, it may be necessary to administer half a baby aspirin to bring some relief.

KEEPING YOUR PUPPY CLEAN

Grooming is part of the daily socialising of your puppy, and again, it is akin to 'topping and tailing' a baby, i.e. cleaning the face and the rear end. Grooming should be a pleasant and therefore therapeutic experience for both dog and owner, and is the ideal way in which to become acquainted. You will need some warm water, more than one piece of sponge or flannel, and a brush and comb.

Start with the face by removing any stale food and debris, and then sponge down with warm water and flannel (or cotton wool which can be discarded). Towel dry, check the eyes for mucous residue which accumulates in the corners, and, if necessary, remove this using a small piece of cotton wool for each eye to avoid transferring infection from one eye to the other.

Gently examine the mouth, and make sure that there is no food stuck between the teeth. If necessary, gently remove the debris. From time to time the teeth should be cleaned, using dog toothpaste, which is readily available in most pet shops. This can be applied by brush or finger, or even with a piece of dental floss.

The Yorkshire Terrier is customarily a docked breed. In other words, the tail has been docked short (in many cases by the breeder) a few days after birth, and as a

The Yorkie's face must be kept clean, gently sponging round the mouth to remove any debris. As your puppy's coat begins to grow, you will need to tie the head coat in a top-knot.

This Yorkie has a good set of adult teeth, but teething can be a trying time for the puppy

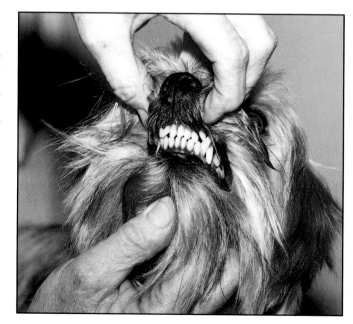

result there is no great problem concerning hygiene as experienced by some of the breeds with long tails. However, docking is now banned in some countries, and we may expect to see an increasing number of Yorkies complete with natural appendages.

It is therefore an essential part of grooming and hygiene to maintain the continued good health and comfort of your pet by checking underneath the tail-end on a daily basis, in order to prevent odour or matting of the hair. The owner must be prepared to swab this end with warm water and disposable material as necessary (baby wipes are ideal for this purpose). If there appears to be any redness, then apply a little Vaseline or some non-astringent cream.

COAT CARE
The Yorkie puppy coat is quite easy to maintain, if grooming is carried out on a regular daily basis. This should be carried out, as with most puppy tasks, at or as near floor level as possible, to avoid the possibility of mishaps. First of all, go over your puppy with your fingers, to comfort and reassure him, and simultaneously to remove tangles, matting and debris, such as twigs or pieces of grass and leaves etc. This should be followed by gently combing the coat through, with a wide-toothed comb, and finally brushing through the coat with a suitable bristle brush.

GROOMING TIPS
1. Keep a firm hold while working with a puppy, as they react very quickly to any new or uncomfortable experience and injury can easily be sustained by a leap from the unsuspecting grasp of child or adult.
2. Work with your puppy at or as near floor level as possible. Sitting on the floor with the puppy on your knee is the ideal way of achieving a rapport, and at this level children learn to participate more easily in a more controllable situation.
3. Use disposable materials, where possible, when matters of hygiene are concerned.
4. Be patient, as a normal healthy puppy can be a handful until he learns to accept being handled.
5. Do not transfer germs from one end of the dog to the other by either tailing first and topping second, or re-using cleaning material and transferring germs from one orifice to another, including eye to eye or ear to ear.

EXERCISE
Your puppy will get enough exercise just by playing in the first months of life, when his energy will be dissipated in frantic bursts, punctuated by periods of rest and sleep. Do not forget that a growing puppy, building muscle, should not be over-stimulated to exhaustion by well-meaning exuberant children. Make sure your puppy always has access to his bed where he can find peace and privacy.

Once the puppy has been fully inoculated, lead training will provide the necessary exercise and stimulus, and then you will be able to enjoy more conventional exercise at your mutual convenience.

LEAD TRAINING
There is a lot to be said for waiting until the puppy is a bit older, has settled into your home and has confidence in you, before you start lead training. You should

begin lead training in the home quite some time before you graduate to the hectic world outside, and you should proceed in easy stages, from home and garden, then to the park, and finally, if possible, a quiet suburban street, before facing the busy shopping precincts with all their attendant hazards.

Start off by giving your puppy a chance to get used to his collar. The best method is to put the collar on for short periods at play time, in order to distract the puppy's attention from the initial resentment he may experience. The pup may attempt to remove this source of irritation by various means, including scratching and rubbing. He should at first be allowed to win these little battles by giving him much praise and removing the collar as soon as he settles down. You will find that the periods when the puppy wears the collar can be quickly extended as he becomes more comfortable and accustomed to something around the neck.

Once this goal has been reached it is time for the next step, which is to encourage your puppy to tolerate the lead attached to his collar. Do not, at this point, attempt to exercise any degree of control or restraint. Eventually, if you get down to eye-level with your small charge, you will be able to take control of the end of the lead and encourage him to approach you, even if this requires some degree of bribery with his favourite morsel of food. Remember there are no prizes for becoming angry or impatient, and you will lose more ground than you gain if you scold or lose your temper.

Give praise and more praise as your puppy improves, and soon he will begin to follow you on a loose lead. By this time you may both feel confident enough to attempt to walk together. This can most satisfactorily be achieved by gradually tightening the tension on the lead, and holding the lead at arm's length away from your body-line, so that puppy is clear of your feet and has plenty of space. Short lessons with praise and reward will make this a pleasure and not a battle, and will result in your puppy feeling secure on his lead before he has to adapt to the distractions of the outside world.

Once you are ready to venture together into the world at large, take short trips to build up your confidence. Allow your pet to become familiar with new sights, sounds and smells. You will encounter people and objects that your puppy is unsure of, so remember that a puppy's first view of the world can be overwhelming, and it is your responsibility to provide the confidence and support he needs at this time. If you take the necessary time and effort, you will be rewarded with the satisfaction of having a safe, happy, well-adjusted companion.

Chapter Four

CARING FOR THE ADULT

FEEDING REGIMES

All growing puppies and adult dogs require a balanced diet, which should consist of the essential vitamins and minerals conducive to good health and growth, irrespective of the particular feeding regime that you choose to adopt to suit your circumstances. Most of the recognised and reputable manufacturers of pet-foods will offer you a choice of either wet or dry foods, which will meet the necessary foregoing criteria, and providing that you study the literature that accompanies these products it becomes largely a matter of personal preference or convenience.

It is perhaps wise to avoid the stronger canned products, such as beef, liver, or heart, which are not always suitable to the Yorkie's digestion, whereas turkey, chicken, rabbit and tripe are to be recommended. Food should always be provided at room temperature, and if it has been frozen, it must always be properly defrosted.

If you decide to provide your pet with food from your own larder, then high on the list are sources of Vitamins A, B, C, D, and E. The main sources of protein are essential, and these are to be found in all dairy products including meat, fish, poultry and game. Most Yorkies love a nice piece of cheese as a special treat, but not as a meal, and milk is generally best avoided as it can cause diarrhoea.

Chicken bones and fish bones should be avoided at all costs, as they can splinter or stick with tragic consequences. Do not feed meat which is too strong or not quite fresh. Your puppy will love a small portion of raw minced beef, and he will probably enjoy most of the cooked food you provide for yourself, including vegetables. Some Yorkies have a passion for fruit. Carbohydrates are also important and these are contained in dog biscuits, meal and cereal products. These will provide the roughage conducive to good health.

If you decide to supplement your Yorkie's diet with additional vitamins, ask your vet for advice as an overdose of some vitamins can end up doing more harm than good. Care should be taken not to over-indulge your pet with tidbits such as cake, chocolate and sweets etc., as this can spoil the appetite, affect the digestion, damage the teeth, and also precipitate gum disease.

QUANTITY

Most proprietary brands of dog food are accompanied by a generally reliable set of instructions, including the amount required relative to the weight of the animal. Initially it is wise to follow the manufacturer's recommendations. However, commonsense and experience will soon teach you how much food your own Yorkie requires, as this can vary considerably depending on the appetite, the lifestyle, and

ABOVE: Yorkies enjoy their food, and you will rarely have a problem with feeding.

LEFT: This nine-year-old bitch still has a good appetite, but as the Yorkie gets older you should make sure the diet is not too rich, and adjust quantity, if necessary, to avoid obesity.

ABOVE:The Yorkie is an adaptable little character and will fit in with his owner's lifestyle, enjoying whatever exercise he is given.

RIGHT: A crate is an invaluable item of equipment, especially if you do a lot of travelling, as the Yorkie has a safe place to settle down when he is in the car.

the size of your pet. Over-feeding should be avoided as obesity can have an adverse effect on the health and life expectancy of the mature pet.

In the first year, quantity is best determined by the appetite of your growing pet, and this can best be assessed by removing food which has not been consumed within about ten minutes of being provided. Try to arrange to feed your pet before you prepare food for the family if you are using a proprietary dog food, as the smell of something you are preparing may be more attractive, resulting in your pet ignoring his own food in the hope of something more exciting. Once this habit is established it can be extremely difficult to overcome.

It is also bad practice to leave a supply of food constantly available, and neither should you feed more than one animal from the same dish at the same time, as you will be unable to ascertain the individual needs of each animal.

PROBLEMS WITH FEEDING

As a rule the Yorkie has a good appetite and will be eager for his food. So if your pet suddenly goes off his food and refuses more than one meal, a visit to the vet is indicated. However, it is not unusual for the healthy pet to regurgitate partly digested food if it has been eaten too quickly. A bitch will sometimes bring food up as part of her natural mothering instincts, which should not be confused with sustained retching of froth or projectile vomiting, indicative of more serious problems which may require urgent veterinary attention.

If your Yorkie appears off-colour, bloated, nauseous, or uncomfortable in respect of digestion, he may instinctively try to make himself sick, which he may do by eating grass. This is not necessarily anything to become instantly alarmed about, if no other symptoms are present. Nevertheless, it may be necessary to monitor his behaviour for twenty-four hours. At the same time, you could provide a liquid diet and a plentiful supply of water and fluids, which gives the digestive system a rest and a chance to recover. If you are taking your Yorkie on a journey it is sensible to take a supply of water with you in order to avoid an upset, which can be caused by a change of water just as much as by a change of food.

THE VETERAN YORKIE

As your Yorkie grows older and becomes less active, his metabolism slows down and he will not require quite as much food as previously. Quantity should therefore be adjusted in order to maintain your pet in good health, and to minimise health problems associated with obesity in the elderly dog, namely poor circulation, chest and heart disease.

The older pet is less able to cope with a rich diet, and with the onset of old age your pet is unlikely to retain full dentition. Those teeth still remaining are likely to be loose, and consequently a slightly more bland and softer diet may be appropriate.

GROOMING AND HYGIENE

Coat care is described in detail in Chapter 5, but there are a number of grooming procedures which involve cleaning and general hygiene which the pet owner should follow in order to keep the Yorkie at the peak of good health.

DIRTY BOTTOMS

This problem is not exclusive to the Yorkie, but the long coat which is characteristic of the breed, does nothing for hygiene in respect of his rear end. It is a quite sensible precaution to keep the coat trimmed short underneath and around the tail if you want to avoid the chore familiar to everyone who has ever owned this breed. For if you are not prepared to wash a dirty bottom, then this is not the breed for you. Every Yorkie owner has, at some time, been panicked by that forlorn look that instantly turns a pet into a dejected soul who appears to be suffering from sudden illness. The owner will then be relieved by the discovery of a dirty bottom, which has usually been caused by the faeces catching in the coat and then being sat upon – at which point, your pet will present the crestfallen appearance of a martyr. Fortunately, this problem is easily resolved with a bowl of warm soapy water, a piece of disposable towelling and a hair-dryer.

EARS
The most common problem with ears is the earmite. This parasite is usually much more prevalent in drop-eared breeds, but it does occur in the Yorkie, mainly as a result of the abundance of hair in and around the ear.

Prevention is generally preferable to the cure, and so the ears should be routinely kept clean and dry, both inside and out. Water must not be allowed to get into the ears, and so when you are bathing your Yorkie, use a mild shampoo on the surface of the ear only.

It may also be necessary to gently pluck out some of the hair at the entrance to the ear, as an aid to ventilation, but you are not encouraged to probe too deeply into the ear. Ear-drops can be used on a regular basis, at least once a month, to protect against the development of ear mite or canker. This can be identified by a foul-smelling brown, sticky discharge from the ear, and is usually accompanied by the dog shaking his head or holding it to the side and scratching at the affected ear. The condition may require veterinary treatment.

EYES
As a rule, the Yorkie does not experience a great deal of trouble with eyes or eyesight. However, because of the profusion of hair which can attract dust and dirt and cause irritation which may develop into conjunctivitis, it is important to make sure that excessive watering, discharge or discomfort is investigated and treated. Treatment by the owner should be restricted to cleaning and bathing the eyes, using one of the many readily available proprietary solutions for the purpose. Alternatively, you can make up your own weak salt solution by adding approximately one teaspoonful of table-salt to a litre of sterile water.

Should an eye problem persist, then veterinary advice should be sought as problems with tear ducts or ingrowing eyelashes will require further treatment.

FEET
The toenails should be kept trimmed short to minimise the risk of damage, as an excessively long nail can curl under the foot and cause extreme discomfort on contact with the ground. This can be done using nail-clippers, making sure that you do not cut into the quick of the nail, which will result in bleeding. Ask your vet, your Yorkie's breeder, or an experienced dog owner to show you how to do this. The hair on the sole of the foot should also be kept trimmed at all times, as a foreign object can become trapped in the matted hair and cause temporary lameness.

A regular check of ears, eyes and nails will help to keep your Yorkie in top condition.

This seventeen-year-old Yorkie has received the best of care throughout his long life from his devoted owner.

TEETH

The adult Yorkie should have forty-two teeth, twenty on the top and twenty-two on the bottom, made up of six incisors top and bottom, four canines, sixteen premolars and ten molars. It is not unusual for some Yorkies not to have a full complement of incisors, which are the front teeth between the two upper and lower fangs or canines. In some cases, there may only be four instead of six, top or bottom, and while this may be unimportant to the pet owner, it may be crucial to the potential exhibitor.

It is a very common occurrence in this breed that when the adult teeth are cut or fully erupted between six and nine months of age, the baby or milk teeth will not be shed naturally and will still be in place, thus presenting a double row of teeth. Food can get trapped in the gap between the two rows of teeth, subsequently harbouring infection. It is therefore essential to have these teeth surgically removed at the earliest opportunity.

In spite of the fact that Yorkies do not lose baby teeth easily, they do lose adult teeth at a relatively young age. The breed is susceptible to disease of both teeth and gums, and you are well advised to pay attention to dental hygiene by regularly cleaning your Yorkie's teeth with one of the many toothpastes available for the purpose. Ask your vet to descale the teeth from time to time, and provide a diet which includes hard biscuit or meal for chewing, as an aid to keeping the teeth firm in the gums.

EXERCISE

The Yorkie is a very sociable and adaptable little character, and his exercise can be suited to your own circumstances. A Yorkie will enjoy outings, and he will be energetic and inquisitive when he is taken out for walk. However, the Yorkie is also the ideal pet for the elderly person, for he will be equally content to share life with the less energetic, as long as he is provided with the stimulus of human company.

Naturally, the older pet will require a decreasing amount of exercise as he loses some of his muscle tone and mobility.

When you are grooming your Yorkie, it is advisable to check both feet and toes to make sure there are no small stones or twigs etc., caught in between toes or matted into the hair of the foot. It is important to remember that although a Yorkie does not require a great deal of exercise, he will benefit from regular exercise on a hard surface. Not only does this help to maintain muscle-tone, it also keeps the toenails buffed short by contact with the abrasive surface. If it is not practical to walk your dog in this manner, then it will be necessary to trim the nails from time to time.

CAR TRAVEL

Car travel is a part of everyday life, and it is important that your Yorkie accepts this form of transport. In most cases, if a Yorkie is properly trained, an outing in the car will be viewed as a treat. When you are preparing to take your puppy for his first journeys in the car, do not feed him before you travel even if you are only going on a short trip, as you will increase the risk of car-sickness. This can quickly turn into a chronic reflex response, which is very difficult to break.

It is also a good plan to establish sensible routines to suit your own convenience while travelling, and then to stick to them so that your puppy learns what is expected at an early age. Endearing lack of discipline in a puppy can very quickly become a source of unacceptable behaviour in an adult dog. Therefore, if the puppy is to travel on your lap, make sure that he does not run loose all over everyone else. Alternatively, if he is to travel in his box or on the back seat, then make sure that this becomes established practice. Never travel with a window open enough to allow your Yorkie to escape, and never allow your dog to travel with his head out of the window. The Yorkshire Terrier makes an ideal travelling companion, and when properly trained, he will happily travel by car, coach or rail, by land, sea or air.

RESPONSIBLE OWNERSHIP

Owning a dog is a big responsibility, and you must ensure that your dog is well integrated in the community you live in. There are a few rules which should always be observed for the well-being of your Yorkie, and for the sake of the community.

1. Make sure your dog is always wearing a collar and is on the lead in public places.
2. Your dog should have some means of identification, such as electronic tagging, tattooing or a disc, giving your address and telephone number, on his collar.
3. Always clean up after your dog in public places.
4. Never leave your dog unattended in a public place.
5. Never leave your dog unattended in a vehicle.

Chapter Five

COAT CARE

THE YORKIE'S COAT

The Yorkshire Terrier's crowning glory is his long, straight flowing coat, with its distinctive steel-blue and tan markings. However, this is the picture presented by the mature show specimen. You should not expect this to apply to the puppy, nor necessarily to the pet Yorkie, unless you intend to keep your pet in show condition. While it is difficult to determine exactly what your puppy's coat will look like as he matures, you will probably want your pet to be a typical representative of the breed. This is why it is important to see the parents, for if they have short, harsh or thick, black, wavy, woolly coats, the puppies may not grow the correct Yorkshire Terrier coat.

When the Yorkie puppy is born it is predominantly black in colour, with tan points above the eyes, and tan markings on the chest and legs. There should be clear definition at the lines of demarcation between the colours. 'Running colour', where the contrasting colours mix, is undesirable and unsightly in the adult animal. As the months pass, the hair on the head should change, first to a sooty colour, then to silver, with a gradual transition to a pale-tan and finally, with maturity, to a glorious golden-shaded tan on the head, face, moustaches and fall. The hair on the ears should be deeper, dark and rich, but more solid tan.

This transition should coincide with the clearing of the puppy coat from black to a dark steel-blue. However, there are a great many variations in colour, texture, and clearing patterns in this breed. There are no absolutes; consequently, it is difficult to be precise. As a general rule, the longer a puppy takes to clear in tan, the darker the body colour is likely to remain. Conversely, the more quickly a puppy clears in tan on the head, the more likely it is that the body coat will change to a lighter silver or blue. Similarly, the heavier or more dense the puppy coat (if it is also soft in texture), the less manageable it is inclined to be as it grows. It may therefore be necessary to consider keeping this type of coat clipped off for ease of maintenance.

The Yorkie coat may come in three distinct types, which would be considered undesirable in a show dog. The pet owner may wish to make an evaluation of coat texture in order to be able to care for the coat, and to know whether is it is possible to keep a particular dog in full coat. The first is the Yorkie with a predominantly black, short and extremely harsh body coat, contrasting with bright ginger markings. This type of coat is very easy to maintain, but it tends to be sparse and will never attain any length as it breaks very easily. The second type is the silver Yorkie with pale-cream coloured face, head and legs, who generally has the most beautiful silken-textured coat. This is easily grown, and is easy to maintain as it seldom breaks

LEFT:When you bath your Yorkie, adjust the temperature of the water so it is hand-warm.

BELOW: Use a towel to soak up the excess moisture, and then you can use a hair-dryer, on a moderate setting, to dry your Yorkie's coat.

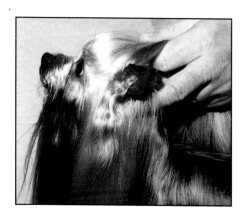

TYING THE TOP-KNOT

ABOVE: Part the hair from the outer corner of the eye in a line backwards to the opening at the base of the ear, on each side of the head.

RIGHT: Brush and gather all the hair upwards to a parting across the head between the ears, and at this central point secure the hair with an elastic-band.

BELOW: Tie the top-knot with a ribbon. If you are going to cracker the coat, you can now start by spraying the hair with an oil-based product such as almond oil.

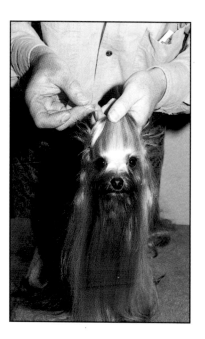

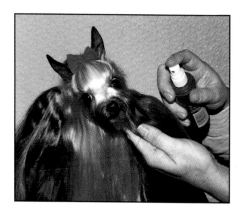

and is easily cultivated. The third extreme is the black, heavy-coated but very pretty type, which is generally of a very soft, woolly texture. This coat mats very easily and is consequently difficult to maintain, unless it is clipped very short. The markings on this type can be various, sometimes a solid mahogany and frequently a pale sooty colour, which never gives way to a clear tan.

GROOMING SESSIONS

It is important to groom your Yorkie on a daily basis, not only for reasons of health and hygiene, but also to build up a rapport with your pet. If you gain his trust, confidence and respect, you will both enjoy the therapeutic benefits of grooming. If you fail to do this, the essential task of caring for your Yorkie's coat becomes nothing more than a chore.

Initially it is a good idea to groom your Yorkie on your lap at floor level, particularly if you lack confidence, or if you do not have someone to help to hold on to your puppy. To begin with, a youngster may resent the indignity of being groomed, restrained or handled. After your puppy has become accustomed to being groomed, you may prefer to progress to a table, in which case precautions are necessary to prevent your dog leaping from the table, until he learns to stand still and enjoy being groomed.

The easiest way to achieve this is to spend a few minutes every day, before you begin grooming, resting your Yorkie on his back on your lap and fussing him, and then standing him on a table for a few minutes while you still have both hands free to restrain him. It will not take long for the Yorkie to become accustomed to this routine.

The amount of effort required to keep your pet tidy and respectable will be determined to some extent by the quantity and texture of the coat. Some Yorkies have a fairly sparse, easily-maintained coat even as adults, while some breeding lines have a much heavier, softer, and less manageable coat, which picks up everything including parasites, twigs and leaves. This type of coat also has a tendency to mat, particularly at the root.

If your Yorkie has a sparse coat, then, apart from the 'topping and tailing' previously described, your dog will need little more than a gentle brush through with a bristle brush, followed by combing the coat to keep it looking neat. As the adult coat grows in and becomes progressively heavier, a bit more time and attention may be required. At this stage, you may decide to keep your Yorkie in a much shorter, more easily managed trim.

THE BODY COAT

Always begin with your Yorkie comfortably settled on his back on your lap and start by grooming underneath, first by removing loose debris from feet, legs and coat with your fingers. At the same time you can check for any cuts or abrasions. Then brush out by holding the hair close to the skin, between thumb and forefinger of one hand (to avoid painful pulling of the hair), and gently tease out matting of the hair with a bristle brush.

Pay particular attention to the legs, neck and chin, and on the stomach always brush forwards towards the head and away from the equipment of the male. Turn the dog over on to his feet or tummy and continue the process with the brush, working your way upwards from the bottom layers of the coat finally reaching the back. This procedure should then be repeated using a fairly wide-toothed comb with smooth round teeth and no sharp edges. Finish by parting the coat along the spine from the base of the skull to the root of the tail.

THE HEAD
Examine the eyes and ears for cleanliness and, if necessary, wipe the eyes with a disposable cloth, moistened with a proprietary brand of eye-bathing solution. Make sure you use a different piece for each eye to avoid transferring infection from one to the other. Then clean the surface of the ears, taking care not to probe beyond the visible part of the ear. From time to time, it may be necessary to apply ear-drops as a preventative measure.

It is desirable, but not essential, to use a smaller baby hairbrush on the head. You should begin by parting the hair from the tip of the nose to the stop between the eyes, and then brushing the moustaches down either side of the face. At first it will only be necessary to brush the hair back away from the face and eyes, but as the hair on the head grows longer it will continually obstruct the vision by falling forward. You will then have to decide (if this is a pet and not a potential show dog) whether to have the hair cut in a fringe, or fastened up with a band or bow.

THE TOP-KNOT
Part the hair from the outer corner of the eye in a line backwards to the opening at the base of the ear, on each side of the head. Then brush and gather all the hair upwards (including the hair between the eyes) to a parting across the head between the ears, and at this central point secure the hair with two or three turns of an elastic band, followed by a clip or bow if desired.

BATHING
There are no hard and fast rules regarding when and how often you should bath a dog, and therefore you should bath your Yorkie as often as you consider necessary. First, gather all the essentials before you begin bathing. This should include a brush, a comb, shampoo, ear-plug material, nail-clippers, a plastic basin to stand the puppy in, one or two warm towels, and a hair-dryer.

The sink is quite a good place to bath your pet, as long as you make sure your puppy does not jump out. The bath is also perfectly acceptable, although there may be too much room for your puppy to struggle. A solution is to use a suitable basin, placed in the sink or bath. A shower unit, if you have one, is perhaps the best place to bath a puppy, as it has the ideal dimensions and height to handle a puppy safely. Make sure your Yorkie has a non-slip mat or even an old heavy towel to stand on. This will help him to feel secure and will stop him from scrabbling.

The water you use for bathing should be adjusted to a suitable hand-warm temperature before you put the puppy in. At the same time, prepare your rinsing water in a suitable container, if you are not using a shower attachment. If you intend using a deep bath or basin, do not put more than a few inches of water in. If there is too much water your puppy is likely to start paddling and splashing furiously in an attempt to swim, and consequently making a terrible mess in the process. Use baby shampoo on your Yorkie's coat as it does not lather or sting too much. It is a good idea to plug the ears with something soft and retrievable to prevent water from getting in.

CRACKERING THE COAT

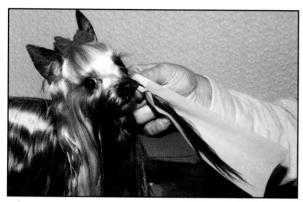

Acid-free tissue paper is used to wrap the coat in papers to protect it from damage. The moustache crackers are put in at either side of the muzzle. Place the paper with the folded edge behind the hair root so that there is no sharp edge to cut the lip and fold the paper around the hair.

Fold the paper up towards the upper lip.

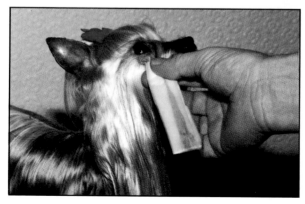

Continue folding, and then secure the paper with a band so that it is not disproportionate in size. It must not stick out sideways or obstruct the eye, nor find its way into the mouth.

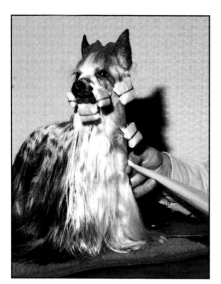

Chin, face and neck crackers are put in before moving down to the chest.

The process continues, with crackers going in the shoulders, ribcage, loin, rump, legs, and top-knot.

All the hard work is worth it when the Yorkie is seen in his full splendour, with long, flowing coat.

Now you are ready to begin your puppy's first bath. Stand him gently in the receptacle, reassuring him, and make sure he is comfortably settled before you start wetting him. Start with the body first, and keep at least one hand on the body at all times (this is where a helping hand comes in useful). Apply a conservative amount of shampoo, and massage this through the body and underside of the coat, legs and feet. Rinse through until the water runs clear, disposing of dirty water as required at this stage. You are now ready to carefully wet the head and face area, making sure you do not get water into the eyes and ears. Repeat the shampoo process, followed by the final rinse as before.

Remove the ear-plugs, and wrap your puppy in a large, soft, warm towel, taking enough time at this stage to let the towel absorb most of the moisture. Do not rub with the towel as this will tangle the coat. Use a fresh towel and pat the head area so it is free of excess water. You are now ready to proceed with the hair-dryer, first ensuring it is on a low heat setting. Start by drying the underside of the body, working from the tail end, and using your fingers to comb through the body coat, and the hair on the legs and the feet. Finally, finish with the head area, avoiding direct heat near the eyes, and making sure you thoroughly dry the ears.

All that remains is to brush your puppy through with his bristle brush. Tell him how clever you have both been, and allow him to watch as you rebuild the kitchen or bathroom! Do not allow your puppy outside until he is properly dry, which can take time, depending on volume of coat. Remember that bathtime is the best time to trim nails, if you are doing this job yourself, as nails are softer after bathing. This is also an ideal opportunity to tidy and trim excess hair from the ears.

EAR TRIMMING

By the time your puppy is three months old, it is reasonable to expect the ears to be erect. If this is not the case, it may be necessary to give them some encouragement, bearing in mind that, if you want to show your dog, the ears must be erect. If you delay too long, you may end up with drop ears. There are various reasons why the ears may never stand erect, such as soft ear leathers, excessive hair on untrimmed ears, very large ears, or poor ear placement, which means low-set on the head – none of which should be confused with the fact that ears may drop while the puppy is teething and then stand up once he cuts his teeth.

If you want to trim your Yorkie's ears, your first task is to remove as much hair as possible from the surface and the edge of the ears. You will require a sharp pair of scissors, and the best time to do it is when puppy is tired and therefore least likely to struggle. Lay the puppy on his back on your lap, take the ear between finger and thumb, and slightly moisten the fringing (hair) around the ear in order to define and locate the edge of the ear.

Then, with the scissors in the other hand, very carefully remove the hair, keeping as close to the edge as you can without risking damage to the ear leather with the scissors. Once you have successfully defined the outline of the ear, turn your attention to the surface, by laying the scissors on the surface of the ear and removing as much hair as you can. This can have the effect of making the ear look much larger than it is, but the procedure is necessary. Once the ears are erect you will only need to remove the hair on the top half-triangle of the ear, which will dramatically improve the appearance. It is possible that within a day or two of carrying out the foregoing procedure, the ears will begin to stand up spontaneously.

If this fails to occur, it may be necessary to take further steps, and your Yorkie's breeder would be the best person to show you how you can do this.

FIXING THE EAR

The best method of doing this is to cut a piece of fairly light card (postcard or cereal packet will suffice) in the shape of the outline of the ear. In other words, shaped like a triangle with slightly curved sides, but make it about 5mm smaller than the outline (circumference) of the ear all round. Next, cut a piece of surgical sticking-plaster exactly the same shape, but only 2mm smaller than the outline of the ear.

Clean the natural oils from the face of the ear by wiping with surgical spirit (make sure to let this dry off), then stick the card to the face of the ear with the tape and leave it in place for about seven days. If the ears are still not erect it may be necessary to repeat this process several times before you get the required result. If this still fails to work, it is fair to assume that, for one reason or another, you have a pet with drop ears.

THE SHOW YORKIE.

The most striking feature of the show Yorkshire Terrier – the most glamorous of all the toy dogs – is the long, flowing, silky coat, but this cannot be achieved without a great deal of dedicated effort by the owner. The result will be determined by a combination of the skill and aptitude of the individual to realise the potential of their particular dog, combined with the temperament of the animal and the capacity to grow sufficient quantity of coat of the correct texture.

There can be no doubt that some Yorkies have a more amenable temperament than others, not only in respect of their show ring presence but also in relation to their attitude and general behaviour. To this end, there are some dogs that will not reach their potential without constant supervision almost twenty-four hours a day, including preventing your show dog from mixing with other dogs, in order to protect the coat from damage by curious and boisterous playmates.

CRACKERING THE COAT

It is readily acknowledged that it is impossible to grow the coat of a Yorkie to the floor, without taking the necessary precautions to protect the coat from various types of damage once it begins to grow. At the front end, damage can be caused by food on the face, by the dog getting his moustaches in his mouth while eating or playing, or simply by scratching or rubbing his face or head, or various other parts of his body. The coat of the male can sustain considerable damage by urine burning the coat when he lifts his leg, and in both sexes the rear end can become soiled when emptying the bowel. The coat can also sustain damage as a result of breaking or splitting at the ends for a number of reasons such as a brittle or dry coat, the coat trailing on the ground, or simply by neglect.

As a rule, the more general grooming instructions referred to earlier are sufficient for the family pet and the puppy up to the age of approximately six months. Crackering (wrapping in papers) should only commence once the coat of the show dog has attained a length where it is potentially at risk, and this will naturally vary from one dog to another. Crackering the coat is a time-consuming business, which requires considerable dexterity and skill. To begin with, you will need to watch an experienced exhibitor at work, before you attempt to take on the task yourself.

Most exhibitors will protect the coat of a show dog from breaking, burning or splitting by applying an oil-based product, such as almond oil, to the ends of the hair and the more vulnerable parts of the coat such as the sides, the tail and the moustaches. Others exhibitors apply a more liberal amount of a stronger or thicker oil or grease to the whole coat. I take the view that less, rather than more, is better, as some more concentrated products can burn the coat and skin. Heavy oil or grease can quickly clog the coat and the pores, causing skin complaints and a necessity for over-frequent bathing or grooming, resulting in the loss of coat.

It is not necessary to put more than top-knot, tail and moustache papers in to begin with, until the rest of the coat gets quite a bit longer at ten to twelve months of age. It can be stressful for a puppy to be put into full crackers all at the one time and I strongly advise you against such a course of action. The most common mistake made by most people is to try to put crackers in a puppy before the coat is long enough or before the puppy is ready to accept them. If the coat is not long enough they will just fall out again, and if the puppy reacts against them he may simply take them out.

This is a process of trial and error, and if you both persevere without falling out with each other, you will eventually be rewarded with success. It is equally wrong to put the crackers in too tight, as this breaks the hair and causes such discomfort that the puppy breaks the rest trying to remove them.

Some dogs, who are inclined to rub or protest at having papers, react favourably to wearing small cotton coats. They seem disinclined to remove the body papers if they cannot get at them, although some coat textures are inclined to mat when the coat is unable to breathe naturally. Once again this can only be determined by trial and error and is therefore a matter of personal preference.

Chapter Six

TRAINING

TIME AND PATIENCE

The time to begin basic obedience training is when your Yorkie is about four months old. Start by teaching your puppy to walk nicely on the lead, to sit, and to come when called. With a little time and patience, you will soon be pleasantly surprised at how clever your Yorkie is, and how quickly he will learn to obey the simple commands involved in basic obedience. At first you may find your puppy is reluctant to walk in a direction that takes you away from home. If this is the case, it may be necessary to make life easier for both of you by walking him on his lead towards home at first until you both gain confidence with the lead.

THE GOLDEN RULES

When you are training your Yorkie, always keep the lessons short so that neither of you gets bored. Give lots of praise and encouragement when appropriate, especially

Despite their size, Yorkies can be trained to compete in mini-agility.

at first, when your pet is less than perfect. Never, ever lose your temper or strike your dog for any reason whatsoever. The Yorkie is a sensitive animal who is desperate to please, and the sound and tone of your voice should be enough to let him know whether or not he has gained your approval.

Animals do not respond to long or inconsistent commands, so keep all words of command short and simple – preferably a single word. It is a good idea to preface your single words of command with your dog's name, in order to gain his attention before issuing the command. The Yorkie, in common with most animals, will respond to lots of love, affection and encouragement. It is important to maintain verbal contact with your dog at all times during training sessions to prevent him from becoming bored and losing interest. If this is combined with sensible discipline and consistency, you will be well rewarded for your efforts. Do not attempt to train your dog unless he is on the lead. The most common mistake an owner can make is to try to teach obedience without using a lead, or trying to get the dog to respond to commands off the lead before he is ready to do so. It is vital that your pet is totally reliable with a command on the lead before you attempt the transition. If, or more likely when, your Yorkie disobeys a command off the lead, do not start nagging him. Put your dog back on the lead and repeat the exercise successfully. Wait until your next training session before you attempt the exercise off the lead again.

LEAD AND COLLAR

Fortunately, basic obedience training is both rewarding and inexpensive, and an appropriate lead and collar are the only items that you will require to make a start. A show lead, which slips over the head, tightens with a sliding bead and does not require a collar, is inappropriate for the purpose of obedience training. Neither should you use a lead that is very short or too heavy.

The best type of lead for the purpose of obedience training is a fairly light webbing lead, with a conventional loop at one end, and at the other a collar-clip with a swivel device to prevent it from becoming twisted up. These can be up to six feet in length, which allows you some slack to distance yourself from your pet when required. This type of lead is light enough to be sensitive, but allows maximum control of your small charge at all times.

The only appropriate collar for obedience training is a light choke chain. Do not be deterred by the name, for the purpose of this type of collar is not to choke your dog, but to use the audible click of the chain in operation to alert him, and to teach him to respond to your commands. You will need the lightest choke chain you can get. It is also extremely important to put this chain on correctly, for if it is fitted incorrectly it will defeat the purpose as it will not be audible, nor will it slacken automatically when tension on the lead is released. The aim is for the chain to run freely at the top of the loop, and then it will release immediately after tightening.

TRAINING CLASSES

You may decide to enrol in one of the many dog training classes, which are generally available in most towns. Some specialise in show and ringcraft training, some specialise in obedience training, and others simply concentrate on teaching both dog and owner sensible behaviour and good manners. Whichever you feel appropriate to your needs, you will be made very welcome at an extremely modest cost. If you decide that you want to become involved in the fascinating and rewarding pastime of competitive obedience training, then you will find that it is possible to participate in obedience tests and trials. These are organised by clubs, which are governed by the rules and regulations of the national Kennel Club. Further information can usually be obtained by contacting a local training club or by applying directly to the Kennel Club.

WALKING TO HEEL

The object of this exercise is to get your Yorkie to walk safely at all times under your control, whether he is on or off the lead. Dogs are always trained to walk to heel on the left hand side, so start with your Yorkie on his lead and chain, sitting at your left side, facing forward. Hold the lead at a comfortable length in your left hand, which you will use to control the position of your dog, and hold the remainder of the lead loosely across your body with the other end of the lead in your right hand.

It will then be necessary to do three things simultaneously: snap the lead with the left hand (causing the lead to click as it tightens), set off walking with your left foot, and give the clear, assertive command "Heel". You should stop after ten paces and praise your Yorkie profusely, and then repeat the exercise for a maximum of ten minutes. As your dog reaches maturity, and you both gain experience, you will be able to extend your training periods in length.

Heelwork should be carried out regularly once or twice a day until your Yorkie gets the idea and automatically sets off at your heel as you start to walk. At first he may want to lag behind or set off ahead, and it will be necessary to correct his position using the lead and the appropriate command: "Heel". To begin with you may need to exert a significant degree of control with the lead. However, the object of the exercise is to gradually reduce the tension on the lead until your dog will walk on a loose lead and respond to the command "Heel" when required to do so. At this point you can begin to practise with your Yorkie off the lead, but only in circumstances where it is safe to do so.

THE SIT

The position for the Sit is the same as the one for the previous exercise. Your Yorkie should be standing adjacent to your left foot with the lead held as before. First, twist the upper part of your body round towards your Yorkie, and transfer the lead from your left to your right hand. Then, place your left hand over your dog's back, with thumb and index finger on either side of the pelvis just in front of the back legs, and give the command "Sit", exerting a steady downwards pressure with the left hand, while keeping an upwards tension on the lead. This will have the effect of making the animal adopt a sitting position.

Hold your Yorkie in this position and repeat the command "Sit" several times, interspersed with praise, encouraging your dog to maintain this position for a few moments. Gradually extend the sitting time before allowing your dog to get up. Repeat the exercise several times over a period of not more than ten minutes. Once again, this exercise should be repeated on a regular daily basis until your Yorkie will respond on a loose lead. At this point it will no longer be necessary to twist round towards your dog, or to transfer the lead to your right hand.

HEEL AND SIT

Once your Yorkie has become proficient in the two previous exercises, you can try

The Yorkie is an intelligent breed, and will respond well to training.

Walking on a lead is an essential requirement for the pet Yorkie, and with a little time and patience your puppy will soon get the idea.

As your Yorkie progresses in his training, you can introduce the Down and the Stay commands

linking them together by giving the command "Sit" every time you come to a halt. Your Yorkie will quickly learn to do this automatically by anticipating the command.

THE STAND

Once your Yorkie is prepared to maintain the sitting position on command, you are ready to progress to the Stand. Once again, the position for the dog while teaching this exercise is adjacent to your left foot, but on this occasion he must be in the newly taught sitting position with the lead in your left hand. The object of this exercise is to teach your Yorkie to move from the Sit to the Stand, on the given command.

Once your Yorkie has learned the Sit, it is a relatively simple exercise to teach your pet to adopt a standing position. This is achieved, as in the previous exercise, by twisting your body round towards your pet while transferring the lead from your left to your right hand. Then, lift your Yorkie's rear end up into the required position with your left hand, giving him the command "Stand".

STAND MEANS STAY

It is important to teach your Yorkie good manners, and to be confident when he is approached or handled by strangers, particularly if he is to become a show dog. You should teach your Yorkie to maintain the Stand position by holding him in the required position, while allowing a friend to run their hands gently over his body. Eventually, you will be able to give the command "Stand", and your Yorkie will stand still on a loose lead and allow himself to be examined. You must intersperse this exercise with plenty of praise and reassurance.

Once you have mastered the Stay, then you can combine the two commands: "Stand" and "Stay", in conjunction with the hand signal for the command "Stay", which is arm extended towards the dog, with palm open and fingers pointing downwards.

THE DOWN

STEP ONE: When you are confident that your Yorkie is reliable with the Sit, you are ready to progress to the Down, which is best achieved by starting with the dog in a sitting position. For this exercise, you should adopt a kneeling position facing your dog. Make sure you gain your Yorkie's confidence in this confrontational position by reassuring him, both verbally and with physical contact.

Then, gently take hold of both front legs, just above the elbows, and as you give the command "Down", lift and draw the legs forwards towards you. This will have the effect of making the dog subside into a lying down position. Naturally, it will be necessary to hold your dog in the Down position until he understands what is required. Once he becomes accustomed to this exercise, you will be able to abandon the confrontational position and move on to the next step.

STEP TWO: When your Yorkie is making some initial progress with the Down, you will soon be able to begin the exercise with the dog sitting adjacent to your left foot. Pass the free end of his lead underneath your left foot and hold it in your right hand, then apply steady pressure on your dog's shoulders with your left hand, give the command "Down", and draw the lead up towards you. This will gently help your dog to assume the lying down position.

As with all exercises, constant repetition with encouragement will soon teach your Yorkie to respond to the verbal command "Down", without the need of physical assistance. At this point, you may prefer to accompany the verbal command with a hand signal, which will eventually be useful when giving commands when you are not in physical contact with the dog. The hand signal for the Down is given by extending the arm towards the dog, palm facing down.

THE STAY

Initially, the object of this exercise is to teach your pet to stay on command in either a sitting or standing position. This is best achieved by starting with your Yorkie in the accustomed sitting position adjacent to your left heel. With the dog in this position and the loose lead in your left hand, take one long pace forward and turn to face the dog. Extend the open right hand, palm facing, with fingers pointing down in front of his face and giving the command "Stay".

At first your Yorkie may try to follow you, as has been his custom. If this happens you should quickly correct him with upward tension on the lead, thus returning him to the sitting position. Reinforce this by repeating the command "Stay", with the correct hand signal. This should be followed by plenty of praise after he has held the position, even for a few seconds. Once your Yorkie understands what is required, you should progress to giving the command and then taking a further step away from him. Build on this, one step at a time, until you can stand behind your dog, or at his side, with the lead at full stretch.

When your Yorkie no longer requires correction by snapping the lead, you can try positioning yourself at a distance of as much as twenty or thirty yards. Some trainers might advise changing the lead and chain for a length of cord or a retractable lead, but I think you should retain the lead and chain that you are both accustomed to and attach the extension to your existing equipment.

When you are satisfied with what you have achieved with the Sit/Stay, you can progress to the Down/Stay. This should be done by starting from the Down command, and thereafter following the same progression.

COME ON COMMAND

This is probably one of the first lessons a puppy should learn, and is best taught as the first part of lead training before he has even learned to walk on the lead. It does not, at first, require snapping of the choke chain or the use of force of any kind, as your Yorkie should respond to gentle persuasion and encouragement because he wants to please you.

Start with your puppy sitting, standing, or lying at the end of the lead, and give a gentle tug on the lead accompanied by the command "Come". In fact, your Yorkie may be so eager to come that his action will precede the command, in which case, give the command and the praise anyway. If the puppy is apprehensive, get down on your knees to his eye level. Do not attempt to drag your puppy towards you, for that will make matters worse. Be patient, and eventually the Yorkie's natural curiosity will overcome his fear, and with plenty of coaxing and praise, he will respond.

As the puppy matures, there should be a natural progression towards a more structured recall. When your Yorkie learns the Sit/Stay, you should be able to stand

Yankee Doodly Dandy of Trisdene (Tristin) qualified for and ran in the agility competition at Crufts in 1990 and 1991 with owner Vanessa Levi.

Trisdene Temptation (Trent), currently the most successful Yorkie competing in top-level agility.

Tristin is one of the smallest dogs to compete in mini-agility.

in front of your dog, facing him. In this position, encourage him to approach you from the sitting position by snapping the lead once, accompanied by the command "Come", and he should know what is required. Once he has learned to obey this command, you should teach him to respond when you adopt various positions to the side and rear of him, and most important, at a distance by using a lead extension.

Only when your Yorkie is reliable under remote control at a distance should you attempt to use the command when he is off the lead. The golden rule about this exercise is not to be tempted to use this command when your dog is running loose off the lead and possibly distracted, for if he learns to disobey when you have no control over him, you may have great difficulty with every other aspect of your obedience training.

Chapter Seven

THE SHOW RING

THE BREED STANDARD

The Breed Standard is a picture in words of what the ideal Yorkshire Terrier should look like. Obviously, the perfect specimen has never been produced, and probably never will be. However, the Breed Standard acts as a guide for breeders, so they know the conformation, temperament, and general appearance that is considered most desirable in their breed. The Standard is also important for judges in the show ring. Their task is to judge the dogs against the 'ideal' presented in the Breed Standard. The dog who wins in the show ring, should be the one who – in the judge's opinion – most resembles the Breed Standard picture and is most typical of the breed. The Standard for each breed is laid down by national Kennel Clubs, and it can be obtained from the relevant bodies on request.

The Yorkshire Terrier is one of the most glamorous of all dogs, with his dainty build, his long flowing coat, and his bright, inquisitive expression, typifying the 'terrier' in his ancestry. Breeders aiming to produce the 'perfect' Yorkie have a number of important points, such as coat texture, colour, conformation etc. to bear in mind. The following is a summary of the Standard to enable the potential owner to identify a specimen which does or does not conform to the relevant criteria. However, it is essential to remember that while a Yorkie may have 'faults' when he is being evaluated by the Breed Standard, this does not detract from his suitability as a family pet and companion.

GENERAL APPEARANCE

The Yorkie should be a very compact and neat little dog (not too long in the back), with an air of confidence, vigour and substance about him belying his size.

TEMPERAMENT

The typical Yorkshire Terrier should be a small, lively, extrovert character with spirit, for he is described as an intelligent toy terrier with an air of importance. You should expect your puppy to be alert, spirited and lively. On no account should he be shy, timid or apprehensive.

COAT AND COLOUR

The hair on the body is required to be reasonably long and perfectly straight. It should reflect the light and be of a fine silky texture. A coat with a wave or a curl is extremely undesirable, as are harsh or soft woollen textured coats. Colour is a subjective opinion, and consequently it is the most contentious issue in the breed.

Everyone in the breed can tell you that your dog should have a dark steel-blue coat, and long, shaded, rich golden tan falls on face, head, chest and legs. However, the colour should not be a silver-blue, and so a darker shade – stopping short of black – is more acceptable.

There should be no tan on the neck. The hair on the chest should be a rich, bright tan, and all tan hair should be darker at the roots than the middle, shading to lighter at the tips. The dark steel-blue body coat should be even in colour, not striped or patchy, and not, under any circumstances, intermingled with hair of any other colour, particularly fawn, bronze, tan, gold, ginger, black or white.

THE HEAD

The Yorkie should have a typical terrier head. The skull should be slightly flattened, and the head should not be too large or round, or long in the muzzle. A pretty head or a kitten face, which some find desirable, is not typical of the breed. The nose should be black, as should the eye-rims and toenails.

The hair of the head should be long, and a rich, golden tan in colour when the Yorkie reaches maturity. The gradual transition of colour goes through various clearing stages from black through to silver, hopefully settling with long golden hair, which should be deeper at the roots shading to a lighter tan in the middle, and lighter still at the tips, especially from the base of the ear and from the muzzle. This gives what is acknowledged as the perfect three-shaded golden tan. The more common faults include a dark sooty strip up the centre of the head from between the eyes, and what are known as 'thumb-prints', which are dark, sooty hairs extending downwards from the base of the ears, or tan colour running down the neck from the base of the skull.

THE EYES

The eyes should be dark (black), sparkling and intelligent. A light eye (brown), although common, is undesirable. The eyes should be placed to look forwards, and a bulging, prominent or bold eye is not desirable. Some people have a preference for a slightly almond-shaped eye, although there is no reference to this in the Standard.

THE EARS

The small, erect 'V' shaped ears should be well placed on the top of the head, and not far apart. Semi-erect ears, soft ears and cropped ears were permissible a century ago, but nowadays these are considered faults which are unacceptable in the show ring. Ears with rounded tips are also to be considered a fault, as are ears which are low-set on the head or located in a ten minutes to two position. The ears should be covered in hair, preferably a very deep rich tan.

THE MOUTH

Particular attention should be given to the mouth, as Yorkies are prone to lose their second teeth while they are still comparatively young. Therefore, good strong teeth set square to the jaw are very desirable. The Breed Standard calls for a "scissor bite", which means that the incisors of the upper jaw should slide neatly past the outside of the lower ones when the teeth are closed on each other. There should not be any crooked or misplaced teeth, there should not be any teeth missing and the jaws should be even. Most judges would also consider an even or level bite to be

The Yorkie's coat is his crowning glory. The body coat should be a dark steel-blue, contrasting with the rich golden tans falls on the face and head.

The judge is looking for a compact, neat little dog, with an air of confidence and vigour, belying his size.

The eyes should be black, sparkling and intelligent, and the ears should be V-shaped and erect.

acceptable, which means that the incisors and the molars in the upper jaw should meet exactly with those of the lower jaw when closed on each other.

Although it is permissible to exhibit a dog which has lost a tooth due to accidental mishap, this should not be confused with the fact that some Yorkies do not produce a full set of incisors top or bottom, and a total of four incisors instead of the required six in each jaw should be considered a serious fault.

THE BODY

The topline or back (spine) should be level when the Yorkie is standing and when he is moving. This means the back should not be humped up or hollowed, and not curving downwards to the tail (which is called a low tail-set). The body should be compact with a curved ribcage (known as a good spring of rib) and not flat (slab) sided. The Yorkie should move freely with a straight driving action, both front and rear, and therefore the shoulders should be well laid back, giving a good reach of neck.

The front legs should be quite straight when viewed from the front, and covered in shaded golden tan (deeper at the roots) no higher than the elbows, which should not stick out. The back legs should be quite straight when viewed from the rear, and they also should be covered in shaded golden tan hair no higher than the stifle, which should be well turned. The feet should be round, neat and compact, and not long or hare-footed.

THE TAIL

The tail is customarily docked, although this may change as anti-docking legislation is being introduced in some countries. The tail should be dark steel-blue in colour, except for a tan flash on the underside. The blue should be a deeper shade at the end of the tail.

WEIGHT

Finally, the weight of the adult show dog should be no more than 7lbs (3.1k). But once again you will have to be guided by the experience of the breeder. Weight need not be a critical factor unless you intend to go into the show ring. Although you may have a personal preference for a smaller pet, don't go for a weak or sickly puppy just because you want a small one. Remember a slightly bigger one may suit a family with energetic and boisterous young children.

SHOW TRAINING

If you intend to show your Yorkie, you will have to wait until he is at least six months of age before you are allowed to enter him for competition. However, you can use this time to teach your Yorkie to behave on a lead, and when he is three or four months old, you can join one of the many training classes that specialise in ring training in order to socialise him with other dogs, and to prepare for his debut in the show ring without putting him under too much pressure.

It is a good idea to join your local Yorkshire Terrier Breed Club, and you can visit one or two shows in order to watch the judging procedure close at hand. British exhibitors at dog shows can also take the opportunity to purchase the requisite show box and a red, pleated box cover from one of the many trade stands. You will also need some red ribbon for your Yorkie's topknot. With this equipment, you can then practise putting the bow in, and standing the puppy in a show pose for short periods until you are both comfortable about this part of the procedure.

You can progress to letting family and visitors speak to your Yorkie and gently handle him while he is being posed. You may even have an experienced doggy friend who will look in his mouth to get him used to having his teeth examined by a judge. This will stand you in good stead when you go to training class, as it is an essential part of the training of a show dog.

At training classes you can expect to meet many different breeds, but it is a good idea to make the acquaintance of and keep company with the toy breeds which are examined on the table, as opposed to the larger breeds which are examined on the floor. While you are waiting to put your dog on the table to be examined, you should practise standing your dog on his box, on a table or on the ground beside other dogs, which is what you will have to do when you go to your first show.

IN THE SHOW RING

In Britain the Yorkie is the only breed that is exhibited on a box. This is a throw-back to the days preceding formal dog showing, when the breed was shown in English public houses which had sawdust on the floors. Yorkies were always shown on a small stool or platform to prevent soiling the coat. Once your Yorkie is on the table you must keep a firm grip on the lead, for your baby may take stage fright and try to leap from the table, but otherwise let the judge take charge. You may be required to hand your brush to the judge so that the coat can be examined. Be prepared to show the mouth (teeth), which hopefully you have already practised at home, although some judges will do this without assistance from you.

Once the dog has been examined you will be required to carry out various walking manoeuvres, which can be practised anywhere once you have learned the basic procedures of handling your dog on the move. In order to show your Yorkie to the best advantage this is normally done by first walking your dog away from the judge in the shape of a triangle, executed in an anti-clockwise direction with the dog on the handler's left. This enables the judge to see the dog's rear action as you walk away, then as you turn left on the second leg, the dog is viewed in profile, and as you complete the third and final leg with a second left turn, you will approach the judge enabling him to see the front of the dog as it comes towards him.

You may be required to walk the dog once up and down, sometimes on a different surface, which is why you should teach your dog to become accustomed to all kinds of surfaces both inside and outside. You must also learn to keep one eye on the dog and the other on the judge for you must keep the dog at all times between yourself and the judge so that the dog can be seen to the best advantage without your legs obstructing the judge's vision. When you change direction, do not lose momentum by letting the dog come to a halt – he must be kept moving. You should always move round the outside of the dog on the turn, even if you have to run to keep up; the novice is always tempted to stand still and let the dog run round the outside. If you are asked to go away from the judge and back again in a straight line, you should do a 'U' turn at the end before coming back towards the judge.

BRITISH SHOWS

There are various types of shows in the UK licensed by the Kennel Club in London. These are: Sanction, Limit, Open, and Championship Shows. The Kennel Club is

Ch. Clantalon Contention: In Britain, the Yorkie is always shown on a red, velvet box.

The skill of the handler is to present the Yorkie so that he shows off all his best points to the judge.

Can. Ch. Curio's Shades of Blueyork making a name for herself in the show ring.

only involved with the choice of judges for Championship shows where Challenge Certificates (CCs) are on offer. In order to become a Champion, a dog must win three CCs under three separate judges. At least one of these CCs must be won after the dog is twelve months old. The Kennel Club is the final court of appeal in any dispute regarding breeding and showing of pedigree dogs.

Only pedigree dogs which are registered with the Kennel Club in London can enter for and exhibit at a dog show licensed by the Kennel Club in the UK. Once your puppy is six months old he can be shown at any show licensed by the Kennel Club, providing there are appropriate classes. The classes for which you may be eligible are clearly included on the forms and eligibility is determined by age and by what the dog has won at any given time in its show career. If you are in any doubt, the secretary of your breed club or the relevant society is the best person to advise you in this respect.

AMERICAN SHOWS

The American Kennel Club (AKC) is the governing body in the USA. It is run on similar lines to the Kennel Club in the UK, although there are one or two essential differences. The British club is composed of individual members, whereas the American counterpart is composed entirely of member clubs. It is also responsible for governing dog events in the USA and for maintaining a registration of pedigree dogs and a stud book. There are something like four thousand clubs in America holding licensed shows, but less than fifteen per cent are actually members of the AKC.

In Britain the Breed Standard for each breed is drawn up by the Kennel Club, who thereafter retain the copyright, whereas in America responsibility for each Breed Standard is in the hands of the relevant Breed Club. The most obvious difference directly affecting the exhibitor is that Champions are made up on a points system. A dog becomes a Champion by winning a total of fifteen points, which are determined by the number of dogs competing and by the area of the country where the points are won. In the course of becoming a Champion, it is also necessary to annex at least two major wins (three, four or five points) under different judges.

Chapter Eight

BREEDING YORKIES

This chapter is not written to encourage the pet owner to start breeding indiscriminately from a bitch who was purchased purely as a pet. The idea of breeding small dogs may be tempting, but, as a rule, it is best left in the hands of the expert who has the experience to cope with any complications that may arise. However, if you decide to breed a litter then, hopefully, this chapter will help you to do so in a competent way, avoiding the many difficulties often experienced by the first-time breeder and the maiden bitch.

WHY BREED A LITTER?
The first question you should ask yourself is why do you want to breed a litter of puppies? One of the most common reasons for mating a bitch is because someone has told you that it is good for the bitch. However, there is no historical evidence to support this view, which is more likely to reflect the maternal aspirations of the owner rather than those of the dog. This can therefore be discounted as a valid reason for breeding.

Another reason for breeding puppies is to make money. In view of the ever-increasing cost of veterinary bills and the small litters normally produced by the Yorkie, I suggest you consider a more viable breed, or better still, find an alternative way of making some money. Another common reason is because the family – or a friend – is so delighted with a particular Yorkie, they want one just the same. In this situation my advice is to buy another puppy from the same source, as it is likely to be less expensive and less harrowing in the long run.

If you are still keen to breed a litter, the next consideration is whether your particular circumstances are conducive to whelping and rearing a litter of puppies. It is not a good idea to leave a pregnant bitch unattended for long periods of time, particularly when the puppies are due to arrive. Emergencies can and do occur, and you would never forgive yourself if your bitch was left unattended in a distressed condition. Puppies frequently do not arrive on schedule, and constant supervision is often necessary before, during, and for some time after the birth. If, for example, the mother is unable to feed the puppies, you would have to attend to this task on an hourly basis until the litter was successfully weaned, which would be at three weeks of age at the earliest.

Finally, you should ask yourself whether you are suited to coping with delivering and rearing a litter of puppies. Remember that once the puppies arrive, there is a great deal of work involved in successfully rearing a litter, which will require constant supervision for anything up to eight weeks before they are ready to go to their new

Choose your breeding stock with care – you have a great responsibility to the breed when you decide to bring new puppies into the world.

Yorkies make good mothers and will take care of all the puppies' needs until they are ready to be weaned.

Attention to cleanliness and hygiene is essential when rearing a litter.

This is a fairly big litter for a Yorkie, but the puppies are evenly matched in size and are clearly thriving.

homes. Do not forget that once puppies are weaned and feeding independently, it is unlikely that mother will clean up after the puppies – and this task will need to be carried out by you.

BREEDING FROM YOUR PET

The breeder and your vet are the two people best equipped to advise on whether you should consider breeding from your pet. If you bought your bitch purely as a pet, it is important to ask the breeder if there is any reason why you should not breed from her. It is absolutely essential that your bitch is a reasonably good representative of the breed, and is sound in temperament. However, the breeder may often sell a puppy which is perfectly satisfactory as a pet, but there may be something about the bitch which precludes her use as a brood. For example, she may be too small, or from a line which has turned out to be poor whelpers, or indifferent mothers. It is obviously preferable if you bought your bitch with the intention of breeding from her, and therefore you will have discussed these matters at the time of purchase.

Assuming that both you and the breeder are in agreement, and you have satisfied yourself regarding the soundness and quality of the line you have purchased, it will then be a question of making sure that your bitch is fit and well when she comes in season. It is therefore sensible to discuss your plans with the vet, in case there is anything relevant to your bitch's health, size, condition or suitability, that, in his opinion, would preclude her from producing a healthy litter.

Nowadays with the advent of the premate test, which can be carried out by your vet, you should be able to establish with certainty exactly when your bitch will ovulate and precisely when she must be mated. Most vets will do a health check and recommend a course of antibiotics at this time, in order to clear up any underlying low-grade infections which may not be immediately apparent. The premate test is a first-class investment, especially, if you have to travel a distance to the stud dog of your choice, as it avoids uncertainty about when the bitch should best be mated.

SELECTING A STUD DOG

Do not wait until your bitch is in season before making enquiries about a stud dog, otherwise the dog you choose may be already booked and you will be forced to make do with an alternative, which is a big disappointment before you have even started. Remember that you will be required to take your bitch to the dog – and not the other way about. While some people send the bitch or leave her with the owner of the stud dog, I do not feel that this is really a very suitable arrangement. It is better to stay with a maiden bitch if you possibly can, rather than leave her in strange surroundings

Remember to discuss the stud fee well beforehand, so that you are not embarrassed about the cost when you arrive with your bitch. You should also discuss the possibility of a double mating (having the bitch mated again a day or so later, just to make sure), which is a good idea when both you and the bitch are inexperienced and might have got your timing slightly wrong. Most breeders are reasonable about this, especially if you are trying to breed for the show ring for the first time. It may even be possible to negotiate a reduction of the fee if the bitch does not produce any puppies. Finally, once you have made arrangements to use a dog, it is good manners to let the owner of the stud dog know as soon as your bitch actually comes into season – you cannot expect to be accommodated at twenty-four hours notice.

When you are choosing a stud dog, the breeder of your bitch is the best person to ask for advice. The breeder will be familiar with the bitch's breeding, and may have an experienced stud dog with suitable breeding. Alternatively, the breeder may be able to introduce you to a suitable dog in your vicinity. An inexperienced maiden bitch may be apprehensive when approached by an unfamiliar dog, and so it is sensible to use an experienced and proven stud dog.

THE IN-SEASON BITCH

It is usual for bitches to come into season every six months, but in the small Toy breeds there are many variations from the norm. Some bitches may have their first season as early as six months, while others could be almost eighteen months old before they come into season. Equally, it is not in the least uncommon for a Yorkie to have only one season a year. It is important to bear in mind that for a small Toy dog, motherhood is a great shock to the system, both mentally and physically. For this reason, you should not mate a bitch in her first season, and you must be satisfied that she is mature enough, both mentally and physically, to rear her litter of puppies.

The first sign that your bitch is about to come into season is when she becomes interesting to male dogs. She may be a bit restless, perhaps fussy about her food, and probably preoccupied with licking at her vulva, which will redden, become puffy then hard, swollen and tender. At this time, your bitch may seek a bit more attention than usual. Keep a close watch over her in the coming days, and you will eventually see a discharge of blood from the vagina, which you should be able to identify from some blood-spotting on her bedding. Your bitch is now in season and will soon be ready for the mating.

The mating should take place between the eleventh and the fourteenth day of the season (which could last anything up to twenty-one days). As the season progresses, the bright-red discharge will decrease and lighten to a pale-pink, and by the eleventh day the hardness and swelling of the vulva will become much softer. At this point, the bitch is ready for mating. She will usually indicate this by flicking her tail to the side and positioning herself to accept the dog, which she will demonstrate if you apply a light pressure with your hand on her back.

THE MATING

The owner of the stud dog will normally take control of the mating, and the most that you will be required to do is to keep a firm hold on your bitch throughout the proceedings. The bitch is unlikely to come to any harm during the proceedings, but the dog is vulnerable to injury if the bitch struggles at the crucial moments.

As there is frequently a disparity in height between the brood bitch and the male of the species (the male frequently being the smaller), it may be necessary to elevate the dog. This can be achieved by folding an old blanket to the requisite thickness and placing it at the rear of the bitch, for the male to stand upon. If your bitch is profuse in coat, it may be advisable to clip or tie back the hair at the rear, in order to more easily accommodate the male.

Most experienced stud dogs will mate the bitch with little or no formality, while other less experienced males may want to play with the bitch to make her acquaintance. Eventually the male will mount the bitch from the rear, and after a few

At three weeks old weaning can begin. It does not take long for a puppy to learn to eat from a dish.

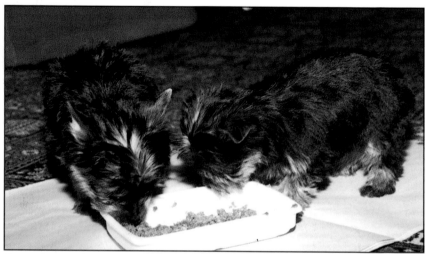

By eight weeks of age the puppies are fully weaned and have gained considerably in size and weight.

A beautifully reared litter of puppies ready to go to their new homes.

tentative exploratory probes to find the target, he will commence thrusting vigorously for a few moments. It is during these and the following proceedings that you must ensure that you keep a firm hold on the bitch, as any sudden movement on her part can result in injury to the male.

Once the male has stopped moving if the mating has been accomplished successfully, he will be unable to immediately withdraw from the bitch. He will remain tied to her for some time until his engorged penis subsides and he can then withdraw. This may only take a few minutes, but more usually both animals will remain in this position for twenty or thirty minutes. A tie is not essential in order for a successful mating to take place, but most breeders feel more confident in the result if this has occurred. After the animals separate, place a piece of tissue over the bitch's vagina and, if possible, keep her rear a bit higher than her head for a time in order to avoid the loss of too much semen.

THE PREGNANT BITCH

The gestation period of the Yorkshire Terrier is sixty-three days. In other words, if your bitch is in whelp (pregnant), the puppies should be born sixty-three days after conception (the mating). However, it is not unusual for the Yorkie bitch to produce her puppies a day or two early, especially if she is heavily in whelp; neither is it unknown for a bitch to be a day or two late. If the puppies have not appeared on cue by the sixty-third day, you should immediately consult your vet in case there is a problem.

Once the bitch has been mated, life can continue as normal for the first four weeks of her pregnancy, with daily exercise and a nourishing diet. It is not easy for the novice to tell if a bitch is pregnant before twenty-eight days. By this time she will begin to put on a little weight around the middle. You may wish to ask the vet to check to see if your bitch is in whelp and is in good health. If she is in whelp, now is the time to provide supplementary feeding. You should offer an extra meal every day, continuing until after the puppies are born and finally weaned. The food should be of the best quality, containing extra protein, vitamins and calcium for the growing pups.

PREPARATIONS

It will be necessary to provide a suitable whelping box some time before your bitch is due to have her puppies so that she can get used to her new accommodation. This should be situated in a warm, quiet corner, well away from other pets and children. It should be of rigid construction, about 3ft (0.85m) square and 18ins (45cm) high, with a hinged lid and a drop-down front, enabling you to work with the bitch when she is delivering the pups, and to fasten them in securely when they are unattended.

The box should have a two-inch by two-inch (5cm by 5cm) wooden rail fastened around the inside circumference, about two inches from the floor. This will prevent the bitch from squashing her puppies if she lies against the side of the box. You will need either a heating-pad for mum and pups to lie on, or an overhead infra-red lamp to keep them warm, as newborn puppies are susceptible to the cold.

You will also need a fairly small cardboard box, lined with a piece of absorbent towelling over a warm water-bottle, in case you need to put new puppies safe while delivering the next one. While you will want to give your bitch something comfortable to lie on, this should be removed when you are delivering the puppies.

The floor of the whelping box should be covered with several thick layers of newspaper so that as these become soiled during whelping they can be peeled away easily to provide a fresh, dry surface.

THE WHELPING

It is not unusual for the pregnant bitch to go off her food a day or two before the arrival of her puppies, and at this time she may also have a loose bowel as she prepares for the birth. This is commonly preceded by a drop in temperature of one or two degrees from 38.6 degrees Centigrade (101.5 Fahrenheit) to 37.2 degrees Centigrade (98.9 Fahrenheit), approximately twenty-four hours before the onset of labour.

The bitch will become increasingly restless and unsettled. She will start to pant, simultaneously scratching and tearing at her bedding until she has shredded the newspaper, which you have so thoughtfully provided. Finally, she will rest quietly for a time as she withdraws into herself and her contractions become apparent. These start with a barely discernible tremor passing in a wave through her body as she lifts her tail, as though straining and then relaxing. Over the next hour or two these spasms will grow stronger and much more pronounced, as the time between each contraction lessens.

Eventually a water sac will appear as the bitch's vagina dilates. Do not panic if this sac, which looks like a small dark liquid-filled balloon, recedes back inside the bitch as she pauses between contractions. In time, the sac will burst, possibly aided by the bitch, and she will expel the first puppy, usually within an hour of the sac appearing or breaking. If a puppy fails to arrive within two hours and the bitch become distressed, you should call for your vet. This also applies if the contractions weaken or cease completely.

Yorkie puppies are not all born head-first, so do not be surprised if some are delivered backwards. If the bitch is exhibiting difficulty finally expelling the partly-delivered puppy (whelp), it may be necessary to carefully grip the protruding whelp with a scrap of towelling, and as the bitch is pushing (and only then), gently but firmly, draw the whelp downwards and under towards her stomach. Hopefully, this will be all that is required to encourage the bitch to produce the other puppies herself.

Once the bitch has expelled the puppy, she may immediately open the sac, sever the cord, and proceed to clean and stimulate the puppy herself. However, you must be prepared to assist her immediately if she seems unsure, as there is not much time to waste. The puppy will arrive encased in a transparent membrane, which may still be attached to the bitch by the umbilical cord. First you must quickly and carefully tear open the membrane with your fingers, although you may need to use a scrap of towelling to get a grip as it is quite slippery. Then clean the mucous from nose and mouth so that the puppy can breathe.

If there is no immediate response, it may be necessary to revive the newborn puppy by patting it dry to stimulate the lungs into action and holding it head downwards to clear any fluid from the lungs. Some bitches attend to this themselves by pushing the whelp about fairly roughly as soon as it is born. Next you must sever the cord an inch or so from the puppy, which can either be done by shredding it with your thumb-nail, taking care not to pull it away from the tummy thus causing a hernia, or by tying the cord with cotton and then cutting the cord with scissors on the side away from the puppy. The afterbirth may then be expelled by the bitch as she delivers the next puppy. You must remember to keep a check on the number of afterbirths expelled, for if one is left inside the bitch it could prove fatal, unless prompt action is taken by the vet, giving an injection to expel the retained debris as soon as possible after the puppies have been born. The bitch is likely to insist on cleaning up after each delivery by devouring the placenta, and this is not to be encouraged as the placenta is a powerful emetic and can severely upset your bitch's digestion.

While the bitch is resting between contractions she may settle down with her first born, but as the next one arrives it may be sensible to place the preceding pups safely out of harm's way in the cardboard box you have prepared. If the whelping is protracted, the bitch should be offered some warm milk or water sweetened with glucose or honey, although this may be rejected until the whelping is complete.

Some puppies will immediately begin to suckle, others may take some time. It may be necessary to help the slower ones by expressing a tiny drop of milk (which may at first be clear) from a nipple and smearing the nipple, and the pup's nose, to encourage him to fasten on. All the puppies should be suckling within an hour or two. Once the bitch has rested for an hour or two, you should offer her fluid with glucose or honey added, and some light food such as scrambled egg to stimulate production of milk. Then, give her the opportunity to empty both bladder and bowel, although she may be reluctant to stay out for long as she will be anxious to attend to her puppies.

ECLAMPSIA

It is important to provide the bitch in whelp with calcium, which should be given on a daily basis in order to maintain good health in the bitch and to build bone in the puppies. It is equally vital to maintain the supply of calcium in the first few weeks while she is feeding her puppies as she is vulnerable to the sudden onset of a condition called eclampsia. This can occur in some mothering bitches with little or no warning. It is caused by depletion of calcium in the blood supply of the nursing mother, and the symptoms are shaking, trembling, panting, and severe muscular spasm and rigidity, which, in the absence of an immediate intravenous injection of calcium, is very quickly fatal.

Fortunately the response to veterinary attention is equally dramatic, and the prognosis usually instant and total recovery. The provision of calcium does not have a cumulative effect, as excess is flushed out in the urine, and therefore the supply must be maintained while the bitch is nursing.

CARING FOR THE PUPPIES

You must be vigilant to make sure that the puppies are feeding properly, especially for the first few days until they are settled. Healthy puppies should be glossy, plump, warm and contented. Cold puppies, which cry constantly, are likely to be in distress and veterinary advice should be sought. In countries where the breed is customarily docked, this is normally done by a vet who will amputate at the extremity of the tan marking on the underside of the tail. It is advisable to have dew claws removed at the same time, and you should make arrangements to have your vet attend to this when the puppies are about four days old. Some of the litter may only have front or rear dewclaws, while others may have none at all.

WEANING

For the first ten days your new charges will do little but eat, sleep and grow, and during this time they will approximately double their birth weight. The eyes and ears begin to open between ten and fifteen days, but sometimes the eyes can be sticky and will benefit from being bathed very gently with tepid water or an eye-wash to encourage them to open. Do not force the eyes open, and do not expose them to bright light. The puppies may not open their eyes at the same time. At first the eyes will have a cloudy bluish tinge; vision will not be complete until the eyes become clear and take on the dark sparkle characteristic of the breed.

The puppies will now become curious and begin to move about more, crawling at first, then sitting up and standing, before finally learning to walk and explore at about three weeks of age. By this time the puppies are beginning to respond to sight, sound and being handled. They should be plump, and the dark, sleek coat should be becoming more profuse. As the puppies grow, they are making increasing demands on mother's resources and at about three to four weeks, as they begin to cut their first teeth, you should begin the weaning process.

Some breeders advocate milk or fluid to start puppies off, but I think the quickest and easiest method is to begin teaching the puppies to lick some honey from your fingers at about two weeks old. Then you can begin the weaning at three and a half weeks, with some raw meat, scraped or very finely minced, on your fingers. The puppies will very quickly learn to lick and suck the meat from your fingers, which is a very short step to feeding from a low, flat dish which should be big enough for them to climb into.

Within a day or two they should be feeding eagerly twice a day from the dish, and at this point you can introduce the messy stage of warm milky cereal, or one of the proprietary puppy weaning products which are readily available. The mother may be anxious to join in, but this should not be allowed as she is likely to eat all the food in sight, and regurgitate it partly-digested for her puppies to eat. This is a perfectly natural response, but it does not aid the weaning process.

This is, therefore, the ideal time to begin to separate the mother from her puppies for progressively longer periods of time. Allow her to come in to her puppies after they have eaten, and she will be more than happy to clean up the puppies and the leftovers. Similarly, it is advisable to start feeding her away from the puppies, to avoid distractions, and to prevent her regurgitating her own food. Keep her away from the litter for about an hour until she has digested her own meal.

Once the puppies are established on the weaning process, you can provide some variety in the feeding in order to stimulate their interest and appetite. Start with scrambled egg, some fish or finely-ground chicken etc. and gradually encourage them to be more and more independent from their mother during the day. Over the next few weeks, the puppies should graduate to eating a well-balanced diet of mainly meat and cereal, approximately four times a day. Finally, as the bitch's milk supply decreases, show the bitch to her own sleeping quarters last thing at night to sleep on her own, so the puppies are fully independent. By this time you should also be starting to feed each puppy separately, in order to ensure that each one is eating a satisfactory amount, commensurate with size and weight, by the time they are six weeks old.

Chapter Nine

HEALTH CARE

The Yorkshire Terrier is quite a tough little dog, despite his tiny size and dainty appearance. With a well-balanced diet, regular exercise and grooming, your Yorkie should have few health problems. However, the owner should be aware of the more common canine ailments in order to give the right treatment. In most cases, it is a matter of spotting problems at an early stage, and then seeking your vet's advice.

ROUTINE CARE

GIVING MEDICATION: It is almost certain that you will, at some time, find it necessary to administer pills, or medicine that your Yorkie does not like. However, this task can be made easier by following these tried and trusted methods.

PILLS: Wrap the pill in a morsel of your Yorkie's favourite treat or hide it in the food at mealtime. However, if this is unsuccessful then put your Yorkie on your knee, and with both hands free (but having the pill immediately to hand), place the left hand over the top of the muzzle so that you can slip the thumb in one side of the mouth at the back of the jaw, and the middle finger in the other side of the mouth. If you apply a slight pressure with these two fingers, it should be enough to encourage your Yorkie to open his mouth wide enough for you to place the pill on the very back of the tongue, almost over the throat, with the thumb and index finger of the right hand (this encourages the swallowing reflex). Finally, hold the mouth closed for a second or two until your dog swallows. The other option is to obtain a small device from your vet, known as a pill-popper, specifically designed for the purpose.

MEDICINE: The easiest way to administer liquid medicine is with a small animal syringe, which can be obtained from your vet specifically for this purpose. Using a similar technique to open the mouth, and with the syringe in the right hand, place the tip of the syringe at the back and side of the mouth, and inject the liquid carefully in small enough amounts to enable your Yorkie to breathe and swallow until the dosage has been satisfactorily administered.

TAKING THE TEMPERATURE: If your dog is sick or listless, or displaying symptoms of fever, it may be necessary to take the temperature. This is achieved by using a rectal thermometer, which is one with a slim end suitable for insertion into the dog's rectum. It may be a good idea to have some assistance, as your Yorkie may try to struggle.

The procedure is to hold the tail up with one hand, while gently inserting the lubricated bulb end of the thermometer, no more than one inch, into the anus with the other hand. The thermometer should be left in place for a minute. When withdrawn, the normal temperature should be 101.5 degrees Fahrenheit (38.6 Centigrade), and any significant departure from this should be treated as abnormal.

BOOSTER VACCINATIONS: Your puppy will receive his first vaccinations at around three months of age, and these provide protection against the major contagious diseases: distemper, parvovirus, hepatitis and leptospirosis. It is essential that protection is maintained throughout your dog's life through an annual booster vaccination, administered by your vet. In some countries a regular vaccination against rabies is also required.

WORMING: It is not unusual for puppies to be born with a roundworm infestation, as the larvae can lie dormant in the mother and be triggered off during pregnancy and subsequently passed to her offspring in the womb. The breeder will have wormed the puppies at least twice before they are ready to go to their new homes. However, it is important that you continue the worming programme, and your vet will advise on this. It is advisable to worm your puppy once a month until he is six months old, and then worm routinely every six months thereafter. Tapeworm, and in some countries, heartworm, can be a problem. Again, seek advice from your vet who will prescribe suitable treatment.

CANINE CONDITIONS AND AILMENTS

ANAL GLANDS: Impaction of the anal glands is not unusual. The condition can be identified by the dog being preoccupied with his rear end, licking or biting as a result of the discomfort, or dragging his rear end along the ground. The anal glands are located underneath the tail on either side of the rectum, and their purpose is to provide a lubricant for the comfortable expulsion of faeces, and also as a scent gland. They are normally stimulated by the roughage in the diet, failing which they may become blocked and require to be drained by your vet.

BLEEDING: Severe bleeding of wounds to the head or body can be temporarily arrested in an emergency by folding a piece of available material into a pad and applying this to the wound using firm pressure. Bleeding from a limb can be controlled by applying a tourniquet between the wound and the body. Care should be taken to ensure that the pressure of the tourniquet is no more than required to control the bleeding, and the pressure will need to be released at frequent intervals.

CHOKING: Some Yorkies are greedy animals, and it is therefore very important to ensure that food is chopped extremely fine to avoid the possibility of choking. If this problem should occur, prompt action is required. The first thing to do is to determine whether you can remove the obstruction by hooking it out with your finger, avoiding at all costs pushing it further down the airway. If this is impossible, then you must quickly turn the dog upside down, holding him by the back legs, first shaking, then swinging the dog, and finally slapping him sharply in an attempt to dislodge the obstruction.

Your puppy will receive his first course of inoculations when he is around three months of age. He will need an annual booster for the rest of his life.

*A healthy
Yorkie will
look keen and
alert, with a
glossy coat and
sparkling eyes.*

*A good diet is
essential in
order to
maintain your
Yorkie in top-
class
condition.
Never over-
feed your dog,
as obesity can
lead to many
health
problems*

COUGHING: This is most often associated with worms infestation, heart complaints or kennel cough, and if persistent it will warrant further investigation by your vet to ascertain the cause.

EARS (STRIPPED LEATHERS): There is a great deal of controversy among both breeders and exhibitors regarding the problem of chronic hair loss from the surface of the ear. This is usually accompanied by a black greasy substance over the surface of the affected ears. In some cases the ears become completely black, with cracks appearing on the surface or the edge of the ear. In the most extreme cases there is a complete disintegration of parts of the periphery, resulting in a serrated appearance to the circumference of the ear which will never regenerate.

The consensus regarding treatment is to keep the ear as clean as possible at all times. Avoid dislodging the hair while doing so, particularly if there is greasy black discoloration to remove. Finally, avoid leaving the surface of the ear devoid of lubricant if there is evidence of a dry crust forming which may culminate in disintegration of the affected area.

In my experience, the problem is more prevalent in the male of the breed and is more likely to be linked to a combination of stress and hormonal imbalance at puberty (ten months). This applies particularly to the more refined Yorkie, who is fine-boned, and has a thin ear leather with subsequent poor blood circulation to the ear, resulting in restricted nourishment of the hair follicles.

FITS: Fits can be caused by such diverse reasons as worm infestation, epilepsy, vitamin deficiency, infections, stress, colic, diabetes, or a drop in the blood sugar level. Therefore, anything resembling a fit warrants full investigation to establish and treat the cause. A fit can be unexpectedly sudden, with little or no warning, or it may be preceded by trembling, salivation, hyper-ventilation, coupled with deterioration of the senses, loss of motor control or muscular spasm, and finally total collapse into unconsciousness with spontaneous loss of control of both bladder and bowel.

Fortunately, the affected dog will usually regain consciousness within a few minutes, although he may require to rest for some time to regain control of all his faculties. At this point he may be light and sound sensitive, and therefore you should not expose your dog to loud noises or bright light for a time.

HEATSTROKE: This is a very serious condition, and it can be fatal in a very short space of time. You should never leave your Yorkie in direct sunlight or unattended in a car for any length of time, as heat can build up in a closed vehicle even in relatively modest temperatures. If you must leave your dog in the car for a short time, make sure it is always parked in the shade, leaving some windows open for adequate ventilation. If the worst happens and you suspect that your Yorkie has been overcome by the heat, the breathing will be laboured and coming in short gasps. The dog will be distressed and in a state of near, or total, collapse. It is essential to lower the body temperature as rapidly as possible by plunging the animal into cold water or applying ice-packs. Immediate veterinary treatment is essential.

LAMENESS
This is one of the most common problems to be found in the Yorkshire Terrier. It is generally confined to the rear legs and can be identified by the affected leg being

carried, or by the animal hopping intermittently. The first step is to check for cuts or injury to the feet, legs or pads, checking between the toes for foreign bodies such as small stones or grass seeds, and examining the toe nails for damage such as a split in a toe nail. If there is no obvious reason, or if there are signs of more serious accidental injury, then the severity and cause mustbe diagnosed by your vet.

PATELLA LUXATION (Slipping Kneecaps): This condition is usually identified as hereditary, although it can be caused or aggravated by an over-exuberant puppy being allowed to jump on and off furniture etc. at an early age. This causes stretching and damaging of the growing ligaments which locate the kneecap, allowing it to slide sideways off the stifle (knee). This results in the sometimes painful or uncomfortable condition identified as slipping patella (kneecap). It is not unusual for a Yorkie to have quite badly slipping kneecaps, and yet to give no indication when he is walking, running or jumping, and clearly not suffering any discomfort.

LEGG PERTHES DISEASE: The classic signs of this hereditary disease are not normally evident in the very young puppy, as the first signs of lameness usually become apparent at about eight to nine months of age. After the onset of the disease, the lameness will normally be persistent and the condition will usually deteriorate over a considerable period of time. Sometimes the condition may appear to stabilise, in which cases the lameness may improve, but it is still possible that the underlying condition may eventually require surgery.

As a rule, an X-ray is necessary to confirm the presence of Legg Perthes disease, which is usually diagnosed at about nine or ten months of age as an hereditary condition of the hip where there is necrosis (disintegration) of the femoral head (the ball) in the hip socket. It is a painful condition ascribed to an inadequate blood supply or an interruption of the blood supply to the head of the femur in the growing stages, resulting in pain and consequent lameness of the affected limb. However, there is a growing body of opinion which suggests that some cases of Legg Perthes can be attributed to trauma (injury), resulting in a temporary interruption to the blood supply to the femur during the growth period of the puppy.

STOMACH PROBLEMS

BOWEL ENTERITIS: An upset tummy is probably the most common and, hopefully, the most temporary of canine complaints, due to the indiscriminate appetite of most animals including the Yorkie. It is also the most obvious and the most alarming, being identified by the symptoms of sickness and diarrhoea. Most cases can be satisfactorily resolved by starving, and providing limited fluids for twenty-four hours. After this, the Yorkie may be restored to a light fish or white meat diet for a day or two, before being re-introduced to a suitably balanced diet.

HAEMORRHAGIC ENTERITIS: If your Yorkie rapidly deteriorates during the first twenty-four hours of developing sickness and diarrhoea, the condition may have become haemorrhagic enteritis, which can indicate canine parvovirus, poisoning, shock or infection. This can be identified by blood in the vomit, or excrement, either of which could be fatal. Give your Yorkie glucose water in order to avoid the rapid onset of dehydration, and immediate emergency veterinary treatment is mandatory.

This ten-year-old male Yorkie has a short pet trim, which is easy to maintain and more comfortable for the dog in his advancing years.

COLIC: This condition can affect both the very young and the very old. When puppies are being weaned they are naturally greedy, and like human babies, they may get a sore tummy as a result of wind. The older Yorkie, with a less elastic bowel, may experience similar discomfort. Both problems can be relieved with a charcoal preparation, accompanied by some gentle massage, to alleviate the abdominal discomfort. Ask your vet for advice.

SKIN COMPLAINTS: Most breeds of dog shed their coat periodically, but the Yorkie is one of the few exceptions to the rule. Therefore, if your dog is losing coat you will need to consult your vet to establish the cause. One of the most likely reasons for loss of coat is the presence of a skin condition, such as an allergy, eczema, mange, or some kind of infestation such as harvest mite, lice or fleas, resulting in itching or discomfort causing the animal to scratch or rub with consequent loss of coat. All of these will respond effectively to veterinary treatment, but they are unlikely to occur if you take the precaution of routinely bathing your Yorkie in a veterinary approved insecticidal shampoo.